TRUTH AND KNOWLEDGE

Wahrheit

und

Wissenschaft.

Vorspiel

einer

„Philosophie der Freiheit"

von

Rudolf Steiner.

Weimar.

Herm. Weissbach.

1892.

TITLE PAGE OF THE FIRST EDITION OF
Truth and Knowledge

TRUTH AND KNOWLEDGE

Introduction to
"Philosophy of Spiritual Activity"

by
Rudolf Steiner

Translated from the German by Rita Stebbing

Edited, and with Notes by Paul M. Allen

STEINERBOOKS

To

DR. EDUARD VON HARTMANN

with the warm regard

of the author

BIBLIOGRAPHICAL NOTE

Rudolf Steiner's *Wahrheit und Wissenschaft* was published by Hermann Weissbach in Weimar, 1892 in a first edition of 1,000 copies.

A second edition of 5,000 copies was published by the Philosophisch-Anthroposophischer Verlag am Goetheanum, Dornach-bei-Basel, Switzerland, 1925.

A third edition of 4,000 copies was published in Freiburg i. Br., Germany, in 1948.

The fourth edition, from which the present translation was made, was issued by the Verlag der Rudolf Steiner-Nachlassverwaltung, Dornach-bei-Basel, Switzerland, 1958, and comprised 4,000 copies.

Thus, the four editions of *Wahrheit und Wissenschaft* published between 1892 and 1958 totaled some 14,000 copies.

In March, 1921 the first English translation of this work appeared in London under the title, *Truth and Science,* translated by Prof. R. F. Alfred Hoernle and edited by Harry Collison.

The present translation is entirely new, having been undertaken especially for the Centennial Edition of the Written Works of Rudolf Steiner.

Additional data concerning the original version of *Wahrheit und Wissenschaft* will be found under note 77 of the Editorial and Reference Notes at the end of this volume.

CONTENTS

Rudolf Steiner

PREFACE

PRESENT-DAY philosophy suffers from an unhealthy faith in Kant.[27] This essay is intended to be a contribution toward overcoming this. It would be wrong to belittle this man's lasting contributions toward the development of German philosophy and science. But the time has come to recognize that the foundation for a truly satisfying view of the world and of life can be laid only by adopting a position which contrasts strongly with Kant's. What did he achieve? He showed that the foundation of things lying beyond the world of our senses and our reason, and which his predecessors sought to find by means of stereotyped concepts, is inaccessible to our faculty of knowledge. From this he concluded that our scientific efforts must be limited to what is within reach of experience, and that we cannot attain knowledge of the supersensible foundation, of the "thing-in-itself." But suppose the "thing-in-itself" and a transcendental ultimate foundation of things are nothing but illusions! It is easy to see that this is the case. It is an instinctive urge, inseparable from human nature, to search for the fundamental nature of things and their ultimate principles. This is the basis of all scientific activity.

There is, however, not the slightest reason for seeking the foundation of things *outside* the given physical and spiritual world, as long as a comprehensive investigation of this world does not lead to the discovery of elements *within* it that clearly point to an influence coming from beyond it.

The aim of this essay is to show that everything necessary to explain and account for the world is within the reach of our thinking. The assumption that there are principles which belong to our world, but lying outside it, is revealed as the prejudice of an out-dated philosophy living in vain and illusory dogmas. Kant himself would have come to this conclusion had he really investigated the powers inherent in our thinking. Instead of this, he shows in the most complicated way that we cannot reach the ultimate principles existing beyond our direct experience, because of the way our faculty of knowledge functions. There is, however, no reason for transferring these principles into another world. Kant did indeed refute "dogmatic" philosophy, but he put nothing in its place. This is why Kant was opposed by the German philosophy which followed. Fichte,[13] Schelling[20] and Hegel[7] did not worry in the least about the limits to cognition erected by Kant, but sought the ultimate principles *within* the world accessible to human reason. Even Schopenhauer, though he maintained that the conclusions of Kant's criticism of reason were eternal and irrefutable truths, found himself compelled to search for the ultimate cause along paths very different from those of Kant. The mistake of these thinkers was that they sought knowledge of the highest truths without having first laid a foundation by investigating the nature of knowledge itself. This is why the imposing edifice of thought erected by Fichte, Schelling and Hegel stands there, so to speak, without foundations. This had a bad effect on the direction taken by the thought of these philosophers. Because they did not understand the significance of the sphere of pure ideas and its relationship to the realm of sense-perceptions, they added mistake to mistake, one-sidedness to one-sidedness. It is no wonder that their all too daring systems could not withstand the fierce opposition of an epoch so ill-disposed toward philosophy; consequently, along with the errors much of real value in their thought was mercilessly swept away.

The aim of the following inquiry is to remedy the lack described above. Unlike Kant, the purpose here is not to show what our faculty of knowledge *cannot* do, but rather to show what it is really able to achieve.

The outcome of what follows is that truth is not, as is usually assumed, an ideal reflection of something real, but is a product of the human spirit, created by an activity which is *free*; this product would exist nowhere if we did not create it ourselves. The object of knowledge is not to *repeat* in conceptual form something which already exists, but rather to *create* a completely new sphere, which when combined with the world given to our senses constitutes complete reality. Thus man's highest activity, his spiritual creativeness, is an organic part of the universal world-process. The world-process should not be considered a complete, enclosed totality without this activity. Man is not a passive onlooker in relation to evolution, merely repeating in mental pictures cosmic events taking place without his participation; he is the active co-creator of the world-process, and cognition is the most perfect link in the organism of the universe.

This insight has the most significant consequences for the laws that underlie our deeds, that is, our moral ideals; these, too, are to be considered not as copies of something existing outside us, but as being present solely *within* us. This also means rejecting the "categorical imperative," an external power whose commandments we have to accept as moral laws, comparable to a voice from the Beyond that tells us what to do or leave undone. Our moral ideals are our own free creations. We have to fulfil only what we ourselves lay down as our standard of conduct. Thus the insight that truth is the outcome of a free deed also establishes a philosophy of morality, the foundation of which is the completely *free personality*.

This, of course, is valid only when our power of thinking penetrates—with complete insight—into the motivating impulses of our deeds. As long as we are not clear about the reasons—either natural or conceptual—for our conduct, we shall experience our motives as something compelling us from outside, even though someone on a higher level of spiritual development could recognize the extent to which our motives originated within our own individuality. Every time we succeed in penetrating a motive with clear understanding, we win a victory in the realm of freedom.

The reader will come to see how this view—especially in its epistemological aspects—is related to that of the most significant philosophical work of our time, the world-view of Eduard von Hartmann.[4]

This essay constitutes a prologue to a *Philosophy of Freedom (The Philosophy of Spiritual Activity)*, a work which will appear shortly.

Clearly, the ultimate goal of all knowledge is to enhance the value of human existence. He who does not consider this to be his ultimate goal, only works as he learned from those who taught him; he "investigates" because that happens to be what he has learned to do. He can never be called "an independent thinker."

The true value of learning lies in the philosophical demonstration of the significance of its results for humanity. It is my aim to contribute to this. But perhaps modern science does not ask for justification! If so, two things are certain: first, that I shall have written a superfluous work; second, that modern scholars are striving in vain, and do not know their own aims.

In concluding this preface, I cannot omit a personal remark. Until now, I have always presented my philosophical views in connection with Goethe's world-view. I was first introduced to this by my revered teacher, Karl Julius Schroer[68] who, in my view, reached such heights as a scholar of Goethe's work because he always looked beyond the particular to the *Idea*.

In this work, however, I hope to have shown that the edifice of my thought is a whole that rests upon its own foundation, and need not be derived from Goethe's world-view. My thoughts, as here set forth, and as they will be further amplified in *The Philosophy of Spiritual Activ-*

ity, have been developed over many years. And it is with a feeling of deep gratitude that I here acknowledge how the friendliness of the Specht family in Vienna, while I was engaged in the education of their children,[69] provided me with an ideal environment for developing these ideas; to this should be added that I owe the final shape of many thoughts now to be found in my *"Philosophy of Spiritual Activity"* to the stimulating talks with my deeply appreciated friend, Rosa Mayreder[70] in Vienna; her own literary works, which spring from a sensitive, noble, artistic nature, presumably will soon be published.

Written in Vienna in the beginning of December 1891.

DR. RUDOLF STEINER

INTRODUCTION

T HE OBJECT of the following discussion is to analyze the act of cognition and reduce it to its fundamental elements, in order to enable us to formulate the problem of knowledge correctly and to indicate a way to its solution. The discussion shows, through critical analysis, that no theory of knowledge based on Kant's line of thought can lead to a solution of the problems involved. However, it must be acknowledged that Volkelt's work,[71] with its thorough examination of the concept of "experience" provided a foundation without which my attempt to define precisely the concept of the "given" would have been very much more difficult. It is hoped in this essay to lay a foundation for overcoming the subjectivism inherent in all theories of knowledge based on Kant's philosophy. Indeed, I believe I have achieved this by showing that the subjective form in which the picture of the world presents itself to us in the act of cognition—prior to any scientific explanation of it—is merely a necessary transitional stage which is overcome in the very process of knowledge. In fact the experience which positivism and neo-Kantianism

advance as the one and only certainty is just the most subjective one of all. By showing this, the foundation is also
laid for objective idealism, which is a necessary consequence of a properly understood theory of knowledge. This
objective idealism differs from Hegel's metaphysical, absolute idealism, in that it seeks the reason for the division
of reality into *given existence* and *concept* in the cognizing subject itself; and holds that this division is resolved,
not in an objective world-dialectic but in the subjective
process of cognition. I have already advanced this viewpoint in *An Outline of a Theory of Knowledge*, 1885,[12] but
my *method* of inquiry was a different one, nor did I analyze the basic elements in the act of cognition as will be
done here.

A list of the more recent literary works which are relevant is given below. It includes not only those works which
have a direct bearing on this essay, but also all those which
deal with related problems. No specific reference is made
to the works of the earlier classical philosophers.

The following are concerned with the theory of cognition in general:

R. Avenarius, *Philosophie als Denken der Welt gemäss dem
    Prinzip des kleinsten Kraftsmasses, usw.,* (Philosophy as
    World-Thinking According to the Principle of the Smallest
    Energy-Mass, etc.) Leipzig, 1876.
———, *Kritik, der reinen Erfahrung* (Criticism of Pure Ex-
    perience) , Vol. I, Leipzig, 1888.
J. F. A. Bahnsen, *Der Widerspruch im Wissen und Wesen der
    Welt,* (The Contradictions in Knowledge and Essense of
    the World) Vol. I, Leipzig, 1882.

J. Baumann, *Philosophie als Orientierung über die Welt*
(Philosophy as Orientation about the World) Leipzig,
1872.

J. S. Beck, *Einzig möglicher Standpunkt, aus welchem die
kritische Philosophie beurteilt werden muss* (The Only
Correct Point of View from which Critical Philosophy
Should be Judged) Riga, 1796.

Friedrich Ed. Benecke, *System der Metaphysik und Religions-
philosophie, usw.,* (System of Metaphysics and Philosophy
of Religion) Berlin, 1839.

Julius Bergmann, *Sein und Erkennen, usw.,* (Existence and
Cognition, etc.) Berlin, 1880.

A. E. Biedermann, *Christliche Dogmatik* (Christian Dogmatics), 2nd Edition, Berlin, 1884-5, Vol. I, pp. 51-173.

H. Cohen, *Kants Theorie der Erfahrung* (Kant's Theory of
Experience) Berlin, 1871.

P. Deussen, *Die Elemente der Metaphysik* (The Elements of
Metaphysics), 2nd Edition, Leipzig, 1890.

W. Dilthey, *Einleitung in die Geisteswissenschaften, usw.,* (In-
troduction to the Spiritual Sciences, etc.) Leipzig, 1883.—Especially the introductory chapters dealing with the interre-
lation of the theory of cognition and the other sciences.—
Further references in works by the same author:
*Beiträge zur Lösung der Frage vom Ursprung unseres
Glaubens an die Realität der Aussenwelt und seinem Recht;
Sitzungsberichte der Kgl. Preuss. Akademic der Wissen-
schaften zu Berlin* (Contributions to the Solution of Our
Belief in the Reality of the Outer World and its Justification. Reports of Meetings of the Royal Prussian Academy
of Sciences in Berlin), Berlin, 1890, p. 977.

A. Dorner, *Das menschliche Erkennen usw.,* (Human Cognition) Berlin, 1887.

E. Dreher, *Ueber Wahrnehmung und Denken* (On Perception
and Thinking), Berlin, 1878.

G. Engel, *Sein und Denken,* (Existence and Thinking) Berlin, 1889.

W. Enoch, *Der Begriff der Wahrnehmung* (The Concept of Perception) , Hamburg, 1890.

B. Erdmann, *Kants Kriticismus in der esten und zweiten Auflage seiner Kritik der reinen Vernunft,* (Kant's Criticism in the First and Second Editions of his Critique of Pure Reason) Leipzig, 1878.

F. v. Feldegg, *Das Gefühl als Fundament der Weltordnung* (Feeling as Fundament of Universal Order) , Vienna, 1890.

E. L. Fischer, *Die Grundfragen der Erkenntnistheorie* (The Basic Questions of the Theory of Cognition) , Mainz, 1887.

K. Fischer, *System der Logik und Metaphysik oder Wissenschaftslehre* (System of Logic and Metaphysics, or Scientific Theory) , 2nd Edition, Heidelberg, 1865.

————, *Geschichte der neueren Philosophie* (History of More Recent Philosophy) , Mannheim, 1860, especially the parts concerning Kant.

A. Ganser, *Die Wahrheit,* (Truth) , Graz, 1890.

C. Göring, *System der kritischen Philosophie,* (System of Critical Philosophy) , Leipzig, 1874.

————, *Ueber den Begriff der Erfahrung* (On the Concept of Experience) , In *Verteiljahrsschrift für wissenschaftliche Philosophie* (Quarterly for Scientific Philosophy) , Leipzig, 1st Year, 1877, p. 384.

E. Grimm, *Zur Geschichte des Erkenntnisproblems, usw.,* (Contribution to the History of the Theory of Cognition) , Leipzig, 1890.

F. Grung, *Das Problem der Gewissheit,* (The Problem of Certainty) , Heidelberg, 1886.

R. Hamerling, *Die Atomistik des Willens,* (The Atomic Theory of Will) , Hamburg, 1891.

F. Harms, *Die Philosophie seit Kant* (Philosophy through Kant) , Berlin, 1876.

E. v. Hartmann, *Kritische Grundlegung des transzendentalen*

Realismus (Critical Establishment of Transcendental Realism) , 2nd Edition Berlin, 1875.

———, *J. H. v. Kirchmanns erkenntnistheoretischer Realismus,* (J. H. v. Kirchmann's Cognitional-Theoretical Realism) , Berlin, 1875.

———, *Das Grundproblem der Erkenntnistheorie, usw.,* (The Fundamental Problem of a Theory of Cognition) , Leipzig, 1889.

———, *Kritische Wanderungen durch die Philosophie der Gegenwart,* (Critical Survey of Contemporary Philosophy) , Leipzig, 1889.

H. L. F. v. Helmholtz, *Die Tatsachen in der Wahrnehmung,* (The Facts of Perception) , Berlin, 1879.

G. Heymans, *Die Gesetze und Elemente des wissenschaftlichen Denkens* (The Laws and Elements of Scientific Thinking) , Leyden, 1890.

A. Hölder, *Darstellung der Kantischen Erkenntnistheorie* (A Presentation of Kant's Theory of Cognition) , Tübingen, 1874.

A. Horwicz, *Analyse des Denkens, usw.,* (Analysis of Thinking) , Halle, 1875.

F. H. Jacobi, *David Hume über den Glauben oder Idealismus und Realismus,* (David Hume on Faith, or Idealism and Realism) , Breslau, 1787.

M. Kappes, *Der "Common Sense" als Prinzip der Gewissheit in der Philosophie des Schotten Thomas Reid* ("Common Sense" as Principle of Certainty in the Philosophy of the Scotsman, Thomas Reid) , Munich, 1890.

M. Kauffmann, *Fundamente der Erkenntnistheorie und Wissenschaftslehre* (Foundations of a Theory of Cognition and Scientific Theory) , Leipzig, 1890.

B. Kerry, *System einer Theorie der Grenzgebiete* (System of a Theory of Border-Areas) , Vienna, 1890.

J. H. v. Kirchmann, *Die Lehre vom Wissen als Einleitung in das Studium philosophischer Werke* (The Theory of Knowl-

edge as Introduction to the Study of Philosophical Works),
Berlin, 1868.

E. Laas, *Die Kausalität des Ich* (The Causality of the I),
Vierteljahrsschrift für wissenschaftliche Philosophie (Quarterly for Scientific Philosophy), Leipzig, 4th Year, 1880, p.
1 ff., 185 ff., 311 ff.

———, *Idealismus und Positivismus* (Idealism and Positivism), Berlin, 1879.

F. A. Lange, *Geschichte des Materialismus* (History of Materialism), Iserlohn, 1873-75.

A. v. Leclair, *Beiträge zu einer monistischen Erkenntnistheorie*
(Studies for a Monistic Theory of Cognition), Breslau, 1882.

———, *Das kategorische Gepräge des Denkens* (The Categorical Mark of Thinking) *Vierteljahrsschrift für wissenschaftliche Philosophie* (Quarterly for Scientific Philosophy),
Leipzig, 7th Year, 1883, p. 257 ff.

O. Liebmann, *Kant und die Epigonen,* (Kant and the
Epigones) Stuttgart, 1865.

———, *Zur Analysis der Wirklichkeit* (Contribution to the
Analysis of Reality), Strassburg, 1880.

———, *Gedanken und Tatsachen* (Thoughts and Facts),
Strassburg, 1882.

———, *Die Klimax der Theorien* (The Climax of the Theories), Strassburg, 1884.

Th. Lipps, *Grundtatsachen des Seelenlebens,* (The Fundamental Facts of Soul Life) Bonn, 1883.

H. R. Lotze, *System der Philosophie, I Teil: Logik* (System of
Philosophy, Part I: Logic), Leipzig, 1874.

J. V. Mayer, *Vom Erkennen* (Concerning Cognition), Freiburg i. Br., 1885.

A. Meinong, *Hume-Studien* (Essays on Hume), Vienna, 1877.

J. St. Mill, *System der induktiven und deduktiven Logik*
(System of Inductive and Deductive Logic), 1843; German
translation, Braunschweig, 1849.

W. Müntz, *Die Grundlagen der Kantschen Erkenntnistheorie*

(Foundation of Kant's Theory of Knowledge), 2nd Edition, Breslau, 1885.

G. Neudecker, *Das Grundproblem der Erkenntnistheorie* (Fundamental Problem of the Theory of Cognition), Nördlingen, 1881.

F. Paulsen, *Versuch einer Entwicklungsgeschichte der Kantschen Erkenntnistheorie* (Study on the History of the Development of the Kantian Theory of Cognition), Leipzig, 1875.

J. Rehmke, *Die Welt als Wahrnehmung und Begriff, usw.*, (The World as Percept and Concept, etc.), Berlin, 1880.

Th. Reid, *Untersuchungen über den menschlichen Geist nach Prinzipien des gesunden Menschenverstandes* (Inquiry into the Human Mind for the Principles of Common Sense), 1764; German translation, Leipzig, 1782.

A. Riehl, *Der philosophische Kritizismus und seine Bedeutung für die positive Wissenschaft* (Philosophical Criticism and its Importance for Positive Science), Leipzig, 1887.

J. Rülf, *Wissenschaft des Weltgedankens und der Gedankenwelt, System einer neuen Metaphysik* (Science of World-Thought and Thought-World, A System of a New Metaphysics), Leipzig, 1888.

R. v. Schubert-Soldern, *Gundlagen einer Erkenntnistheorie* (Fundamentals of a Theory of Cognition), Leipzig, 1884.

G. E. Schulze, *Aenesidemus*, Helmstädt, 1792.

W. Schuppe, *Zur voraussetzungslosen Erkenntnistheorie* (Contribution to a Theory of Cognition Free of Presuppositions), *Philosophische Monatschefte* (Philosophical Monthly), Berlin, Leipzig, Heidelberg, 1882, Vol. XVIII, Nos. 6 and 7.

Rud. Seydel, *Logik oder Wissenschaft vom Wissen* (Logic, or the Science of Knowledge), Leipzig, 1866.

Christoph v. Sigwart, *Logik* (Logic), Freiburg i. Br., 1878.

A. Stadler, *Die Grundsätze der reinen Erkenntnistheorie in der Kantischen Philosophie* (The Principles of the Pure Theory of Cognition in the Philosophy of Kant), Leipzig, 1876.

H. Taine, *De l'Intelligence*, 5th Edition, Paris, 1888.

A. Trendelenburg, *Logische Untersuchungen* (Logical Researches), Leipzig, 1862.

F. Ueberweg, *System der Logik* (System of Logic), 3rd Edition, Bonn, 1882.

H. Vaihinger, *Hartmann, Dühring, Lange*, Iserlohn, 1876.

Th. Varnbühler, *Widerlegung der Kritik der reinen Vernunft* (Refutation of the Critique of Pure Reason), Leipzig, 1890.

J. Volkelt, *Immanuel Kants Erkenntnistheorie, usw.*, (Immanuel Kant's Theory of Cognition, etc.), Hamburg, 1879.

———, *Erfahrung und Denken* (Experience and Thinking), Hamburg, 1886.

Richard Wahle, *Gehirn und Bewusstsein* (Brain and Consciousness), Vienna, 1884.

W. Windelband, *Präluden* (Preludes), Freiburg i. Br., 1884.

———, *Die verschiedenen Phasen der Kantschen Lehre vom "Ding an sich"* (The Various Phases of Kant's Theory of the "Thing-in-Itself") *Vierteljahrsschrift für wissenschaftliche Philosophie* (Quarterly for Scientific Philosophy), Leipzig, 1st Year (1877), p. 224 ff.

J. H. Witte, *Beiträge zur Verständnis Kants* (Contirbutions to the Understanding of Kant), Berlin, 1874.

———, *Vorstudien zur Erkenntnis des unerfahrbaren Seins* (Preliminary Studies for the Cognition of Non-Experienceable Existence), Bonn, 1876.

H. Wolff, *Ueber den Zusammenhang unserer Vorstellungen mit Dingen ausser uns* (On the Correlation of our Perceptions with Things Outside Ourselves), Leipzig, 1874.

Joh. Wolff, *Das Bewusstsein und sein Objekt* (Consciousness and its Object), Berlin, 1889.

W. Wundt, *Logik* (Logic), Vol. I: *Erkenntnislehre* (Theory of Cognition), Stuttgart, 1880.

The following titles related to Fichte:

F. C. Biedermann, *De Genetica philosophandi ratione et methodo, praesertim Fichtii, Schellingii, Hegelii, Dissertationis particula prima, syntheticam Fichtii methodum exhibens,* etc., Lipsiae, 1835.

F. Frederichs, *Der Freiheitsbegriff Kants und Fichtes* (The Concept of Freedom of Kant and Fichte), Berlin, 1886.

O. Gühloff, *Der transcendentale Idealismus* (Transcendental Idealism), Halle, 1888.

P. Hensel, *Ueber die Beizehung des reinen Ich bei Fichte zur Einheit der Apperception bei Kant* (On the Relation between the Pure I in the Works of Fichte and the Unity of Perception in those of Kant), Freiburg i. Br., 1885.

G. Schwabe, *Fichtes und Schopenhauers Lehre vom Willen mit ihren Consequenzen für Weltbegreifung und Lebensführung* (The Theory of Will of Fichte and Schopenhauer and its Consequences for Understanding the World and the Conduct of Life), Jena, 1887.

The numerous works published on the occasion of Fichte's Anniversary in 1862 are of course not included here. However, I would, above all, mention the Address of Trendelenburg (A. Trendelenburg, *Zur Erinnerung an J. G. Fichte*—To the Memory of J. G. Fichte—Berlin, 1862), which contains important theoretical viewpoints.

TRUTH AND KNOWLEDGE

PRELIMINARY REMARKS

E PISTEMOLOGY is the scientific study of what all other sciences presuppose without examining it: *cognition* itself. It is thus a philosophical science, fundamental to all other sciences. Only through epistemology can we learn the value and significance of all insight gained through the other sciences. Thus it provides the foundation for all scientific effort. It is obvious that it can fulfil its proper function only by making no presuppositions itself, as far as this is possible, about man's faculty of knowledge. This is generally accepted. Nevertheless, when the better-known systems of epistemology are more closely examined it becomes apparent that a whole series of presuppositions are made at the beginning, which cast doubt on the rest of the argument. It is striking that such hidden assumptions are usually made at the outset, when the fundamental problems of epistemology are formulated. But if the essential problems of a science are misstated, the right solution is unlikely to be forthcoming. The history of science shows that whole epochs have suffered from innumerable mistakes which can be traced to the simple fact that certain problems were wrongly formulated. To illustrate this, we need not go back as far as Aristotle's physics[73] or Raymond Lull's *Ars Magna*;[74] there are plenty of more recent examples. For instance, innumerable problems concerning the purpose of rudimentary organs of certain organisms could only be rightly formulated when the condition for doing so had first been created through the discovery of the fundamental law of biogenesis.[75] While biology was influenced by teleological views, the relevant problems could not be formulated in a way which could lead to a satisfactory answer. For example, what fantastic ideas were entertained concerning the function of the pineal gland in the human brain, as long as the emphasis was on its purpose! Then comparative anatomy threw some light on the matter by asking a different question; instead of asking what the organ was "for," inquiry began as to whether, in man, it might be merely a remnant from a lower level of evolution. Another example: how many physical questions had to be modified after the discovery of the laws of the mechanical equivalent of heat and of conservation of energy![76] In short, success in scientific research depends essentially on whether the problems can be formulated rightly. Even though epistemology occupies a very special place as the basis presupposed by the other sciences, nevertheless, successful progress can only be expected when its fundamental problems are correctly formulated.

The discussion which follows aims so to formulate the problem of cognition that in this very formulation it will do full justice to the essential feature of epistemology, namely, the fact that it is a science which must contain no presuppositions. A further aim is to use this philosophical basis for science to throw light on Johann Gottlieb Fichte's philosophy of science.[77] Why Fichte's attempt in particular to provide an absolutely certain basis for the sciences is linked to the aims of this essay, will become clear in due course.

KANT'S BASIC EPISTEMOLOGICAL QUESTION

Κ<small>ANT IS GENERALLY CONSIDERED</small> to be the founder of epistemology in the modern sense. However, the history of philosophy *before* Kant contains a number of investigations which must be considered as more than mere *beginnings* of such a science. Volkelt points to this in his standard work on epistemology, saying that critical treatments of this science began as early as Locke.[78] However, discussions which to-day come under the heading of epistemology[79] can be found as far back as in the philosophy of ancient Greece. Kant then went into every aspect of all the relevant problems, and innumerable thinkers following in his footsteps went over the ground so thoroughly that in their works or in Kant's are to be found repetitions of all earlier attempts to solve these problems. Thus where a *factual* rather than a *historical* study of epistemology is concerned, there is no danger of omitting anything important if one considers only the period since the appearance of Kant's *Critique of Pure Reason*.[80] All earlier achievements in this field have been repeated since Kant.

Kant's fundamental question concerning epistemology

is: *How are synthetical judgments a priori possible?* Let us consider whether or not this question is free of presuppositions. Kant formulates it because he believes that we can arrive at certain, unconditional knowledge only if we can prove the validity of synthetical judgments a priori. He says:

"In the solution of the above problem is comprehended at the same time the possibility of the use of pure reason in the foundation and construction of all sciences which contain theoretical knowledge a priori of objects."[81] "Upon the solution of this problem depends the existence or downfall of the science of metaphysics."[82]

Is this problem as Kant formulates it, free of all presuppositions? Not at all, for it says that a system of absolute, certain knowledge can be erected only on a foundation of judgments that are synthetical and acquired independently of all experience. Kant calls a judgment "synthetical" where the concept of the predicate brings to the concept of the subject something which lies completely outside the subject—"although it stands in connection with the subject,"[83] by contrast, in analytical judgment, the predicate merely expresses something which is already contained (though hidden) in the subject. It would be out of place here to go into the extremely acute objections made by Johannes Rehmke[84] to this classification of judgments. For our present purpose it will suffice to recognize that we can arrive at true knowledge only through judgments which add one concept to another in such a way that the content of the second was not already contained—at least *for us*—in the first. If, with Kant, we wish to call this category of judgment *synthetical,* then it must be agreed that knowledge in the form of judgment can only be attained when the connection between predicate and subject is synthetical in this sense. But the position is different in regard to the second part of Kant's question, which demands that these judgments must be acquired a priori, i.e., independent of all experience. After all, it is conceivable that such judgments might not exist at all. A theory of knowledge must leave open, to begin with, the question of whether we can arrive at a judgment solely by means of experience, or by some other means as well. Indeed, to an unprejudiced mind it must seem that for something to be independent of experience in this way is impossible. For whatever object we are concerned to know, we must become aware of it directly and individually, that is, it must become experience. We acquire mathematical judgment too, only through *direct experience* of particular single examples. This is the case even if we regard them, with Otto Liebmann[85] as rooted in a certain faculty of our consciousness. In this case, we must say: This or that proposition must be valid, for, if its truth were denied, consciousness would be denied *as well;* but we could only grasp its content, as knowledge, through experience in exactly the same way as we experience a process in outer nature. Irrespective of whether the content of such a proposition contains elements which guarantee its absolute validity or whether it is certain for other reasons, the fact remains that we cannot make it our own unless at some stage it becomes experience for us. This is the first objection to Kant's question.

The second consists in the fact that at the beginning of a theoretical investigation of knowledge, one ought not to maintain that no valid and absolute knowledge can be obtained by means of experience. For it is quite conceivable that experience itself could contain some characteristic feature which would guarantee the validity of insight gained by means of it.

Two presuppositions are thus contained in Kant's formulation of the question. One presupposition is that we need other means of gaining knowledge besides experience, and the second is that all knowldge gained through experience is only approximately valid. It does not occur to Kant that these principles need proof, that they are open to doubt. They are prejudices which he simply takes over from dogmatic philosophy and then uses as the basis of his critical investigations. Dogmatic philosophy assumes them to be valid, and simply uses them to arrive at knowledge accordingly; Kant makes the same assumptions and merely inquires under what conditions they are valid. But suppose they are not valid at all? In that case, the edifice of Kant's doctrine has no foundation whatever.

All that Kant brings forward in the five paragraphs preceding his actual formulation of the problem, is an attempt to prove that mathematical judgments are synthetical (an attempt which Robert Zimmermann,[86] if he does not refute it, at least shows it to be highly questionable). But the two assumptions discussed above are retained as scientific prejudices. In the *Critique of Pure Reason*[87] it is said:

"Experience no doubt teaches us that this or that object is constituted in such and such a manner, but not that it could not possibly exist otherwise." "Experience never exhibits strict and absolute, but only assumed and comparative universality (by induction) ."

In *Prolegomena*[88] we find it said:

"Firstly, as regards the *sources* of metaphysical knowledge, the very conception of the latter shows that these cannot be empirical. Its principles (under which not merely its axioms, but also its fundamental conceptions are included) must consequently never be derived from experience, since it is not *physical* but *metaphysical* knowledge, i.e., knowledge beyond experience, that is wanted."

And finally Kant says:

"Before all, be it observed, that proper mathematical propositions are always judgments *a priori*, and not empirical, because they carry along with them the conception of necessity, which cannot be given by experience. If this be demurred to, it matters not; I will then limit my assertion to *pure* mathematics, the very conception of which implies that it consists of knowledge altogether non-empirical and a priori."[89]

No matter where we open the *Critique of Pure Reason* we find that all the investigations pursued in it are based on these dogmatic principles. Cohen[90] and Stadler[91] attempt to prove that Kant has established the a priori nature of mathematical and purely scientific principles. However, all that the *Critique of Pure Reason* attempts to show can be summed up as follows: Mathematics and pure natural science are a priori sciences; from this it follows that the form of all experiences must be inherent in the subject itself. Therefore, the only thing left that is empirically given is the material of sensations. This is built up into a system of experiences, the form of which is inherent in the subject. The formal truths of a priori theories have meaning and significance only as principles which regulate the material of sensation; they make experience possible, but do not go further than experience. However, these formal truths are the synthetical judgment a priori, and they must—as condition necessary for experience—extend as far as experience itself. The *Critique of Pure Reason* does not at all prove that mathematics and pure science are a priori sciences but only establishes their sphere of validity, *pre-supposing* that their truths are acquired independently of experience. Kant, in fact, avoids discussing the question of proof of the a priori sciences in that he simply excludes that section of mathematics (see conclusion of Kant's last statement quoted above) where even in his own opinion the a priori nature is open to doubt; and he limits himself to that section where he believes proof can be inferred from the concepts alone. Even Johannes Volkelt finds that:

"Kant starts from the positive assumption that a necessary and universal knowledge exists as an actual fact." "These presuppositions which Kant never specifically attempted to prove, are so contrary to a proper critical theory of knowledge that one must seriously ask oneself whether the *Critique of Pure Reason* is valid as critical epistemology."

Volkelt does find that there are good reasons for answering this question affirmatively, but he adds: "The critical conviction of Kant's theory of knowledge is nevertheless seriously disturbed by this dogmatic assumption."[92] It is evident from this that Volkelt, too, finds that the *Critique of Pure Reason* as a theory of knowledge, is not free of presuppositions.

O. Liebmann, Hölder, Windelband, Ueberweg, Ed. v. Hartmann[93] and Kuno Fischer,[94] hold essentially similar views on this point, namely, that Kant bases his whole argument on the *assumption* that knowledge of pure mathematics and natural science is acquired a priori.

That we acquire knowledge independently of all experience, and that the insight gained from experience is of general value only to a limited extent, can only be conclusions derived from some other investigation. These assertions must definitely be preceded by an examination both of the nature of experience and of knowledge. Examination of experience could lead to the first principle; examination of knowledge, to the second.

In reply to these criticisms of Kant's critique of reason, it could be said that every theory of knowledge must first lead the reader to where the starting point, free of all presuppositions, is to be found. For what we possess as knowledge at any moment in our life is far removed from this point, and we must first be led back to it artificially. In actual fact, it is a necessity for every epistemologist to come to such a purely didactic arrangement concerning the starting point of this science. But this must always be limited merely to showing to what extent the starting point for cognition really is the absolute start; it must be presented in purely self evident, analytical sentences and, unlike Kant's argument, contain no assertions which will influence the content of the subsequent discussion. It is also incumbent on the epistemologist to show that his starting point is really free of all presuppositions. All this, however, has nothing to do with the nature of the starting point itself, but is quite independent of it and makes no assertions about it. Even when he begins to teach mathematics, the teacher must try to convince the pupil that certain truths are to be understood as axioms. But no one would assert that the *content* of the axioms is made dependent on these preliminary considerations.* In exactly the same way the epistemologist must show in his introductory remarks how one can arrive at a starting point free of all presuppositions; yet the actual content of this starting point must be quite independent of these considerations. However, anyone who, like Kant, makes definite, dogmatic assertions at the very outset, is certainly very far from fulfilling these conditions when he introduces his theory of knowledge.

---

* In the chapter titled "The Starting Point of Epistemology," I shall show to what extent my discussion fulfils these conditions.

iii

EPISTEMOLOGY SINCE KANT

ALL PROPOUNDERS of theories of knowledge since Kant have been influenced to a greater or lesser degree by the mistaken way he formulated the problem of knowledge. As a result of his "a priorism" he advanced the view that all objects given to us are our *representations*. Ever since, this view has been made the basic principle and starting point of practically all epistemological systems. The only thing we can establish as an immediate certainty is the principle that we are aware of our representations; this principle has become an almost universally accepted belief of philosophers. As early as 1792 G. E. Schulze maintained in his *Aenesidemus*[95] that all our knowledge consists of mere representations, and that we can never go beyond our representations. Schopenhauer,[96] with a characteristic philosophical fervor, puts forward the view that the enduring achievement of Kantian philsophy is the principle that the world is "my representation." Eduard von Hartmann[97] finds this principle so irrefutable that in his book, *Kritische Grundlegung des transzendentalen Realismus* (Critical Basis of Transcendental Realism) he

39

assumes that his readers, by critical reflection, have overcome the naive identification of the perceptual picture
with the thing-in-itself, that they have convinced themselves of the *absolute diversity* of the subjective-ideal content of consciousness—given as perceptual object through
the act of representing—and the thing existing by itself,
independent both of the act of representing and of the
form of consciousness; in other words, readers who have
entirely convinced themselves that the totality of what is
given us directly consists of our *representations*.[98] In his
final work on epistemology, Eduard von Hartmann did attempt to provide a foundation for this view. The validity
of this in relation to a theory of knowledge free from presuppositions, will be discussed later. Otto Liebmann[99]
claims that the principle: "Consciousness cannot jump beyond itself" must be the inviolable and foremost principle
of any science of knowledge. Volkelt is of the opinion that
the first and most immediate truth is: "All our knowledge
extends, to begin with, only as far as our representations";
he called this the most positive principle of knowledge,
and considered a theory of knowledge to be "eminently
critical" only if it "considers this principle as the sole
stable point from which to begin all philosophizing, and
from then on thinks it through consistently."[100] Other
philosophers make other assertions the center of epistemology, e.g.: the essential problem is the question of the
relation between thinking and existence, as well as the
possibility of meditation between them,[101] or again: How
does that which exists become conscious, (Rhemke) etc.
Kirchmann starts from two epistemological axioms: "the

perceived is" and "the contradictory is not."[102] According to E. L. Fischer[103] knowledge consists in the recognition of something *factual* and *real*. He lays down this dogma without proof as does Göring, who maintains something similar: "Knowledge always means recognizing something that exists; this is a fact that neither scepticism nor Kantian criticism can deny."[104] The two latter philosophers simply lay down the law: This they say is knowledge, without judging themselves.

Even if these different assertions were correct, or led to a correct formulation of the problem, the place to discuss them is definitely not at the beginning of a theory of knowledge. *For they all represent at the outset a quite specific insight into the sphere of knowledge.* To say that my knowledge extends to begin with only as far as my representations, is to express a quite definite judgment about cognition. In this sentence I add a predicate to the world given to me, namely, its existence in the form of representation. But how do I know, *prior to all knowledge,* that the things given to me are *representations?*

Thus this principle ought not to be placed at the foundation of a theory of knowledge; that this is true is most easily appreciated by tracing the line of thought that leads up to it. This principle has become in effect a part of the whole modern scientific consciousness. The considerations which have led to it are to be found systematically and comprehensively summarized in Part I of Eduard von Hartmann's book, *Das Grundproblem der Erkenntnistheorie* (The Fundamental Problem of Epistemology). What is advanced there can thus serve as a kind of guide when discussing the reasons that led to the above assumption.

These reasons are physical, psycho-physical, physiological, as well as philosophical.

The physicist who observes phenomena that occur in our environment when, for instance, we perceive a sound, is led to conclude that these phenomena have not the slightest resemblance to what we directly perceive as sound. Out there in the space surrounding us, nothing is to be found except vibrations of material bodies and of air. It is concluded from this that what we ordinarily call sound or tone is solely a subjective reaction of our organism to those wave-like movements. Likewise it is found that light, color and heat are something purely subjective. The phenomena of color-diffraction, refraction, interference and polarization show that these sensations correspond to certain transverse vibrations in external space, which, so it is thought, must be ascribed partly to material bodies, partly to an infinitely fine elastic substance, the ether. Furthermore, because of certain physical phenomena, the physicist finds himself compelled to abandon the belief in the continuity of objects in space, and to analyze them into systems of minute particles (molecules, atoms) the size of which, in relation to the distance between them, is immeasurably small. Thus he concludes that material bodies affect one another across empty space, so that in reality force is exerted from a distance. The physicist believes he is justified in assuming that a material body does not affect our senses of touch and warmth by direct contact, because there must be a certain distance, even if very small, between the body and the place where it touches the skin. From this he concludes further that what we sense as the hardness or warmth of a body, for example, is only the reaction of the peripheral nerves of our senses of touch and warmth to the *molecular forces* of bodies which act upon them across empty space.

These considerations of the physicist are amplified by those of the psycho-physicist in the form of a science of specific sense-energies. J. Müller[105] has shown that each sense can be affected only in a characteristic manner which is conditioned by its structure, so that it always reacts in the same way to any external stimulus. If the optic nerve is stimulated, there is a sensation of light, whether the stimulus is in the form of pressure, electric current, or light. On the other hand, the same external phenomenon produces quite different sensations, according to which sense organ transmits it. This leads to the conclusion that there is only *one* kind of phenomenon in the external world, namely motion, and that the many aspects of the world which we perceive derive essentially from the reaction of our senses to this phenomenon. According to this view, we do not perceive the external world itself, but merely the subjective sensations which it releases in us.

Thus physiology is added to physics. Physics deals with the phenomena occurring outside our organism to which our perceptions correspond; physiology aims to investigate the processes that occur in man's body when he experiences a certain sense impression. It shows that the epidermis is completely insensitive to external stimuli. In order to reach the nerves connected with our sense of touch on the periphery of the body, an external vibration must first be transmitted through the epidermis. In the case of hearing and vision the external motion is further modified through a number of organs in these sense-tools, before it reaches the corresponding nerve. These effects, produced in the organs at the periphery of the body, now have to be conducted through the nerve to the central organ, where sensations are finally produced through purely mechanical processes in the brain. It is obvious that the stimulus which acts on the sense organ is so changed through these modifications that there can be no similarity between what first affected the sense organs, and the sensations that finally arise in consciousness. The result of these considerations is summed up by Hartmann in the following words:

"The content of consciousness consists fundamentally of the sensations which are the soul's reflex response to processes of movement in the uppermost part of the brain, and these have not the slightest resemblance to the molecular movements which called them into being."

If this line of thought is correct and is pursued to its conclusion, it must then be admitted that our consciousness does not contain the slightest element of what could be called external existence.

To the physical and physiological arguments against so-called "naive realism" Hartmann adds further objections which he describes as essentially philosophical. A logical examination of the first two objections reveals that in fact one can arrive at the above result only by first assuming the existence and interrelations of external things, as ordinary naive consciousness does, and then investigating how this external world enters our consciousness by means of our organism. We have seen that between receiving a sense impression and becoming conscious of a sensation, every trace of such an external world is lost, and all that remains in consciousness are our representations. We must therefore assume that our picture of the external world is built up by the soul, using the material of sensations. First of all, a spatial picture is constructed using the sensations produced by sight and touch, and sensations arising from the other senses are then added. When we are compelled to think of a certain complex of sensations as connected, we are led to the concept of matter, which we consider to be the carrier of sensations. If we notice that some sensations associated with a substance disappear, while others arise, we ascribe this to a change regulated by the causal laws in the world of phenomena. According to this view, our whole world-picture is composed of subjective sensations arranged by our own soul-activity. Hartmann says: "Thus all that the subject perceives are modifications of its own soul-condition and nothing else."[106]

Let us examine how this conviction is arrived at. The argument may be summarized as follows: If an external world exists then we do not perceive it as such, but through our organism transform it into a world of representations. When followed out consistently, this is a self-cancelling assumption. In any case, can this argument be used to establish any conviction at all? Are we justified in regarding our given world-picture as a subjective content of representations, just because we arrive inevitably at this conclusion if we start from the assumption made by naive consciousness? After all, the aim was just to prove this assumption invalid. It should then be possible for an assertion to be wrong, and yet lead to a correct result. This can happen, but the result cannot then be said to have been *proved* by the assertion.

The view which accepts the reality of our directly given picture of the world as certain and beyond doubt, is usually called naive realism. The opposite view, which regards this world-picture as merely the content of our consciousness, is called transcendental idealism. Thus the preceding discussion could also be summarized as follows: *Transcendental idealism demonstrates its truth by using the same premises as the naive realism which it aims to refute.* Transcendental idealism is justified if naive realism is proved incorrect, but its incorrectness is only demonstrated by means of the incorrect view itself. Once this is realized there is no alternative but to abandon this path and to attempt to arrive at another view of the world. Does this mean proceeding by trial and error until we happen to hit on the right one? That is Hartmann's approach when he believes his epistemological standpoint established on the grounds that his view explains the phenomena, whereas others do not. According to him the various world-views are engaged in a sort of struggle for existence in which the fittest is ultimately accepted as victor. But the inconsistency of this procedure is immediately apparent, for there might well be other hypotheses which would explain the phenomena *equally* satisfactorily. For this reason we prefer to adhere to the above argument for the refuting of naive realism, and investigate precisely where its weakness lies. After all, naive realism is the viewpoint from which we all start. It is therefore the proper starting-point for a critical investigation. By recognizing its shortcomings we shall be led to the right path much more surely than by simply trusting to luck.

The subjectivism outlined above is based on *the use of thinking* for elaborating certain facts. This presupposes that, starting from certain facts, a correct conclusion can be obtained through logical thinking (logical combination of particular observations). But the *justification* for using thinking in this way is not examined by this philosophical approach. This is its weakness. While naive realism begins by assuming that the content of experience, as we perceive it, is an objective reality without examining if this is so, the standpoint just characterized sets out from the equally uncritical conviction that thinking can be used to arrive at scientifically valid conclusions. In contrast to naive realism, this view could be called naive rationalism. To justify this term, a brief comment on the concept of "naive" is necessary here. A. Döring[107] tries to define this concept in his essay, *Ueber den Begriff des naiven Realismus* (Concerning the Concept of naive Realism). He says:

"The concept 'naive' designates the zero point in the scale of reflection about one's own relation to what one is doing. A naive content may well be correct, for although it is unreflecting and therefore simply non-critical or uncritical, this lack of reflection and criticism excludes the objective assurance of truth, and includes the possibility and danger of error, yet by no means necessitates them. One can be equally naive in one's

life of feeling and will, as in the life of representing and
thinking in the widest sense; furthermore, one may express
this inner life in a naive manner rather than repressing and
modifying it through consideration and reflection. To be
naive means not to be influenced, or at least not consciously
influenced by tradition, education or rules; it means to be, in
all spheres of life, what the root of the word: 'nativus' implies,
i.e., unconscious, impulsive, instinctive, daimonic."

Starting from this, we will endeavor to define "naive"
still more precisely. In all our activities, two things must
be taken into account: the activity itself, and our knowledge of its laws. We may be completely absorbed in the
activity without worrying about its laws. The artist is in
this position when he does not reflect about the laws according to which he creates, but *applies* them, using feeling and sensitivity. We may call him "naive." It is possible, however, to observe oneself, and enquire into the
laws inherent in one's own activity, thus abandoning the
naive consciousness just described through knowing exactly the scope of and justification for what one does. This
I shall call *critical.* I believe this definition comes nearest
to the meaning of this concept as it has been used in
philosophy, with greater or lesser clarity, ever since Kant.
Critical reflection then is the opposite of the naive approach. A critical attitude is one that comes to grips with
the laws of its own activity in order to discover their re-
liability and limits. Epistemology can only be a critical
science. For its object is an essentially subjective activity
of man: *cognition,* and it wishes to demonstrate the
laws inherent in cognition. Thus everything "naive" must

be excluded from this science. Its strength must lie in doing precisely what many thinkers, inclined more toward the practical doing of things, pride themselves that they have never done, namely, "think about thinking."

iv

THE STARTING POINT OF EPISTEMOLOGY

As we have seen in the preceding chapters, an epistemological investigation must begin by rejecting existing
knowledge. Knowledge is something brought into existence by man, something that has arisen through his activity. If a theory of knowledge is really to explain the *whole*
sphere of knowledge, then it must start from something
still quite untouched by the activity of thinking, and what
is more, from something which lends to this activity its
first impulse. This starting point must lie outside the act
of cognition, it must not itself be knowledge. But it must
be sought *immediately* prior to cognition, so that the very
next step man takes beyond it is the *activity of cognition*.
This absolute starting point must be determined in such
a way that it admits nothing already derived from cognition.

Only our *directly given world-picture* can offer such a
starting point, i.e. that picture of the world which presents
itself to man *before* he has subjected it to the processes of
knowledge in any way, before he has asserted or decided
anything at all about it by means of thinking. This "di-

rectly given" picture is what flits past us, disconnected, but still undifferentiated.* In it, nothing appears distinguished from, related to, or determined by, anything else. At this stage, so to speak, no object or event is yet more important or significant than any other. The most rudimentary organ of an animal, which, in the light of further knowledge may turn out to be quite unimportant for its development and life, appears before us with the same claims for our attention as the noblest and most essential part of the organism. *Before* our conceptual activity begins, the world-picture contains neither substance, quality nor cause and effect; distinctions between matter and spirit, body and soul, do not yet exist. Furthermore, any other predicate must also be excluded from the world-picture at this stage. The picture can be considered neither as reality nor as appearance, neither subjective nor objective, neither as chance nor as necessity; whether it is "thing-in-itself," or mere representation, cannot be decided at this stage. For, as we have seen, knowledge of physics and physiology which leads to a classification of the "given" under one or the other of the above headings, cannot be a basis for a theory of knowledge.

If a being with a fully developed human intelligence were suddenly created out of nothing and then confronted the world, the *first* impression made on his senses and his thinking would be something like what I have just characterized as the directly given world-picture. In practice, man never encounters this world-picture in this form at

---

* Differentiation of the given, indistinct, world picture into distinct entities is already an act of thought activity.

any time in his life; he never experiences a division between a purely passive awareness of the "directly-given" and a thinking recognition of it. This fact could lead to doubt about my description of the starting point for a theory of knowledge. Hartmann says for example:

"We are not concerned with the hypothetical content of consciousness in a child which is just becoming conscious or in an animal at the lowest level of life, since the philosophizing human being has no experience of this; if he tries to reconstruct the content of consciousness of beings on primitive biogenetic or ontogenetic levels, he must base his conclusions on the way he experiences his own consciousness. Our first task, therefore, is to establish the content of man's consciousness when he begins philosophical reflection."[108]

The objection to this, however, is that the world-picture with which we begin philosophical reflection already contains predicates mediated through cognition. These cannot be accepted uncritically, but must be carefully removed from the world-picture so that it can be considered free of anything introduced through the process of knowledge. This division between the "given" and the "known" will not in fact, coincide with any stage of human development; the boundary must be drawn *artificially*. But this can be done at every level of development so long as we draw the dividing line correctly between what confronts us free of all conceptual definitions, and what cognition subsequently makes of it.

It might be objected here that I have already made use of a number of conceptual definitions in order to extract from the world-picture as it appears when completed by man, that other world-picture which I described as the directly given. However, what we have extracted by means of thought does not characterize the directly given world-picture, nor define nor express anything about it; what it does is to guide our attention to the dividing line where the starting point for cognition is to be found. The question of truth or error, correctness or incorrectness, does not enter into this statement, which is concerned with the moment preceding the point where a theory of knowledge begins. It serves merely to guide us *deliberately* to this starting point. No one proceeding to consider epistemological questions could possibly be said to be standing at the starting point of cognition, for he already possesses a certain amount of knowledge. To remove from this all that has been contributed by cognition, and to establish a pre-cognitive starting point, can only be done conceptually. But such concepts are not of value as knowledge; they have the purely negative function of removing from sight all that belongs to knowledge and of leading us to the point where knowledge begins. These considerations act as signposts pointing to where the act of cognition first appears, but at this stage, do not themselves form part of the act of cognition. Whatever the epistemologist proposes in order to establish his starting point raises, to begin with, no question of truth or error, but only of its suitability for this task. From the starting point, too, all error is excluded, for error can only begin with cognition, and therefore cannot arise *before* cognition sets in.

Only a theory of knowledge that starts from considerations of this kind can claim to observe this last principle.

For if the starting point is some object (or subject) to which is attached any conceptual definition, then the possibility of error is already present in the starting point, namely in the definition itself. Justification of the definition will then depend upon the laws inherent in the act of cognition. But these laws can be discovered only in the course of the epistemological investigation itself. Error is wholly excluded only by saying: I eliminate from my world-picture all conceptual definitions arrived at through cognition and retain only what enters my field of observation without any activity on my part. When on principle I refrain from making any statement, I cannot make a mistake.

Error, in relation to knowledge, i.e. epistemologically, *can occur only within the act of cognition.* Sense deceptions are not errors. That the moon upon rising appears larger than it does at its zenith is not an error but a fact governed by the laws of nature. A mistake in knowledge would occur only if, in using thinking to combine the given perceptions, we misinterpreted "larger" and "smaller." But this interpretation is part of the act of cognition.

To understand cognition exactly in all its details, its origin and starting point must first be grasped. It is clear, furthermore, that what *precedes* this primary starting point must not be included in an explanation of cognition, but must be presupposed. Investigation of the essence of what is here presupposed, is the task of the various branches of scientific knowledge. The present aim, however, is not to acquire specific knowledge of this or that element, but to investigate cognition itself. Until we have understood the act of knowledge, we cannot judge the significance of statements about the content of the world arrived at through the *act of cognition*.

This is why the directly given is not defined as long as the relation of such a definition to what is defined is not known. Even the concept: "directly given" includes no statement about what precedes cognition. Its only purpose is to point to this given, to turn our attention to it. At the starting point of a theory of knowledge, the concept is only the first initial relation between cognition and world-content. This description even allows for the possibility that the total world-content would turn out to be only a figment of our own "I," which would mean that extreme subjectivism would be true; subjectivism is not something that *exists* as *given*. It can only be a conclusion drawn from considerations based on cognition, i.e. it would have to be confirmed by the theory of knowledge; it could not be assumed as its basis.

This directly given world-content includes everything that enters our experience in the widest sense: sensations, perceptions, opinions, feelings, deeds, pictures of dreams and imaginations, representations, concepts and ideas.

Illusions and hallucinations too, at this stage are equal to the rest of the world-content. For their relation to other perceptions can be revealed only through observation based on cognition.

When epistemology starts from the assumption that all the elements just mentioned constitute the content of our consciousness, the following question immediately arises: How is it possible for us to go beyond our consciousness and recognize actual existence; where can the leap be made from our subjective experiences to what lies beyond them? When such an assumption is not made, the situation is different. Both consciousness and the representation of the "I" are, to begin with, only parts of the directly-given and the relationship of the latter to the two former must be discovered by means of cognition. Cognition is not to be defined in terms of consciousness, but vice versa: both consciousness and the relation between subject and object in terms of cognition. Since the "given" is left without predicate, to begin with, the question arises as to how it is defined at all; how can any start be made with cognition? How does one part of the world-picture come to be designated as perception and the other as concept, one thing as existence, another as appearance, this as cause and that as effect; how is it that we can separate ourselves from what is objective and regard ourselves as "I" in contrast to the "not-I?"

We must find the bridge from the world-picture as given, to that other world-picture which we build up by means of cognition. Here, however, we meet with the following difficulty: As long as we merely stare passively at the given we shall never find a point of attack where we can gain a foothold, and from where we can then proceed with cognition. Somewhere in the given we must find a place where we can set to work, where something exists which is akin to cognition. If everything were really *only* given, we could do no more than merely stare into the external world and stare indifferently into the inner world of our individuality. We would at most be able to *describe* things as something external to us; we should never be able to *understand* them. Our concepts would have a purely external relation to that to which they referred; they would not be inwardly related to it. For real cognition depends on finding a sphere somewhere in the given where our cognizing activity does not merely presuppose something given, but finds itself active in the very essence of the given. In other words: precisely through strict adherence to the given as merely given, it must become apparent that not everything *is* given. Insistence on the given alone must lead to the discovery of something which goes beyond the given. The reason for so insisting is not to establish some arbitrary starting point for a theory of knowledge, but to discover the true one. In this sense, the *given* also includes what *according to its very nature is not-given.* The latter would appear, to begin with, as *formally* a part of the given, but on closer scrutiny, would reveal its true nature of its own accord.

The whole difficulty in understanding cognition comes from the fact that we ourselves do not create the content of the world. If we did this, cognition would not exist at all. I can only ask questions about something which is given to me. Something which I create myself, I also *determine myself,* so that I do not need to ask for an explanation for it.

This is the second step in our theory of knowledge. It consists in the postulate: In the sphere of the given there must be something in relation to which our activity does not hover in emptiness, but where the content of the world itself enters this activity.

The starting point for our theory of knowledge was placed so that it completely *precedes* the cognizing activity, and thus cannot prejudice cognition and obscure it; in the same way, the next step has been defined so that there can be no question of either error or incorrectness. For this step does not prejudge any issue, but merely shows what conditions are necessary if knowledge is to arise at all. It is essential to remember that it is we ourselves who postulate what characteristic feature that part of the world-content must possess with which our activity of cognition can make a start.

This, in fact, is the only thing we can do. For the world-content as given is completely undefined. No part of it of its own accord can provide the occasion for setting it up as the starting point for bringing order into chaos. The activity of cognition must therefore issue a decree and declare what characteristics this starting point must manifest. Such a decree in no way infringes on the quality of the given. It does not introduce any arbitrary assertion into the science of epistemology. In fact, it asserts nothing, but claims only that if knowledge is to be made explainable, then we must look for some part of the given which can provide a starting point for cognition, as described above. If this exists, cognition can be explained, but not otherwise. Thus, while the given provides the general starting point for our theory of knowledge, it must now be narrowed down to some particular point of the given.

Let us now take a closer look at this demand. Where, within the world-picture, do we find something that is not

merely given, but only given insofar as it is being produced in the actual act of cognition?

It is essential to realize that the activity of producing
something in the act of cognition must present itself to us
as something also directly given. It must not be necessary
to draw conclusions before recognizing it. This at once
indicates that sense impressions do not meet our require-
ments. For we cannot know directly but only indirectly
that sense impressions do not occur without activity on our
part; this we discover only by considering physical and
physiological factors. But we do know absolutely directly
that concepts and ideas appear only in the act of cognition
and through this enter the sphere of the directly given. In
this respect concepts and ideas do not deceive anyone. A
hallucination may appear as something externally given,
but one would never take one's own concepts to be something given without one's own thinking activity. A lunatic
regards things and relations as real to which are applied
the predicate "reality," although in fact they are not real;
but he would never say that his concepts and ideas entered
the sphere of the given without his own activity. It is a
characteristic feature of all the rest of our world-picture
that it must be *given* if we are to experience it; the only
case in which the opposite occurs is that of concepts and
ideas: *these we must produce if we are to experience them.*
Concepts and ideas alone are given us in a form that
could be called *intellectual seeing.* Kant and the later
philosophers who follow in his steps, completely deny this
ability to man, because it is said that all thinking refers
only to objects and does not itself produce anything. In

intellectual seeing the content must be contained within the thought-form itself. But is this not precisely the case with pure concepts and ideas? (By concept, I mean a principle according to which the disconnected elements of perception become joined into a unity. Causality, for example, is a concept. An idea is a concept with a greater content. Organism, considered quite abstractly, is an idea.) However, they must be considered in the form which they possess while still quite free of any empirical content. If, for example, the pure idea of causality is to be grasped, then one must not choose a particular instance of causality or the sum total of all causality; it is essential to take hold of the pure concept, Causality. Cause and effect must be sought in the world, but before we can discover it in the world we ourselves must first produce *causality* as a thought-form. If one clings to the Kantian assertion that of themselves concepts are empty, it would be impossible to use concepts to determine anything about the given world. Suppose two elements of the world-content were given: a and b. If I am to find a relation between them, I must do so with the help of a principle which has a definite content; I can only produce this principle myself in the act of cognition; I cannot derive it from the objects, for the definition of the objects is only to be obtained by means of the principle. Thus a principle by means of which we define objects belongs entirely to the conceptual sphere alone.

Before proceeding further, a possible objection must be considered. It might appear that this discussion is unconsciously introducing the representation of the "I," of the "personal subject," and using it without first justifying it. For example, in statements like "we produce concepts" or "we insist on this or that." But, in fact, my explanation contains nothing which implies that such statements are more than turns of phrase. As shown earlier, the fact that the act of cognition depends upon and proceeds from an "I," can be established only through considerations which themselves make use of cognition. Thus, to begin with, the discussion must be limited to the act of cognition alone, without considering the cognizing subject. All that has been established thus far is the fact that something "given" exists; and that somewhere in this "given" the above-described postulate arises; and lastly, that this postulate corresponds to the sphere of concepts and ideas. This is not to deny that its source is the "I." But these two initial steps in the theory of knowledge must first be defined in their pure form.

v

COGNITION AND REALITY

Concepts and ideas, therefore, comprise part of the given and at the same time lead beyond it. This makes it possible to define what other activity is concerned in attaining knowledge.

Through a postulate we have separated from the rest of the given world-picture a particular part of it; this was done because it lies in the nature of cognition to start from just this particular part. Thus we separated it out only to enable us to understand the act of cognition. In so doing, it must be clear that we have artificially torn apart the unity of the world-picture. We must realize that what we have separated out from the given has an essential connection with the world content, irrespective of our postulate. This provides the next step in the theory of knowledge: it must consist in restoring that unity which we tore apart in order to make knowledge possible. The act of restoration consists in *thinking* about the world as given. Our thinking consideration of the world brings about the actual union of the two parts of the world-content: the part we survey as given on the horizon of our

63

experience, and the part which has to be produced in the act of cognition before that can be given also. The act of cognition is the synthesis of these two elements. Indeed, in every single act of cognition, one part appears as something produced within that act itself, and, through the act, as added to the merely given. This part, in actual fact, is always so produced, and only appears as something given at the beginning of epistemological theory.

To permeate the world, as given, with concepts and ideas, *is* a *thinking* consideration of things. Therefore, thinking is the act which mediates knowledge. It is only when thinking arranges the world-picture by means of its own activity that knowledge can come about. Thinking itself is an activity which, in the moment of cognition, produces a content of its own. Therefore, insofar as the content that is cognized issues from thinking, it contains no problem for cognition. We have only to observe it; the very nature of what we observe is given us directly. A *description* of thinking is also at the same time the science of thinking. Logic, too, has always been a description of thought-forms, never a science that proves anything. Proof is only called for when the content of thought is synthesized with some other content of the world. Gideon Spicker is therefore quite right when he says in his book, *Lessings Weltanschauung*, (Lessing's World-View), page 5, "We can never experience, either empirically or logically, whether thinking in itself is correct." One could add to this that with thinking, all proof ceases. For proof presupposes thinking. One may be able to prove a particular fact, but one can never prove proof as such. We can only describe what a proof is. In logic, all theory is pure empiricism; in the science of logic there is only observation. But when we want to know something other than thinking, we can do so only with the help of thinking; this means that thinking has to approach something given and transform its chaotic relationship with the world-picture into a systematic one. This means that thinking approaches the given world-content as an organizing principle. The process takes place as follows: Thinking first lifts out certain entities from the totality of the world-whole. In the given nothing is really separate; everything is a connected continuum. Then thinking relates these separate entities to each other in accordance with the thought-forms it produces, and also determines the outcome of this relationship. When thinking restores a relationship between two separate sections of the world-content, it does not do so arbitrarily. Thinking waits for what comes to light of its own accord as the result of restoring the relationship. And it is this result alone which is knowledge of that particular section of the world content. If the latter were unable to express anything about itself through that particular relationship established by thinking, then this attempt made by thinking would fail, and one would have to try again. All knowledge depends on man's establishing a correct relationship between two or more elements of reality, and comprehending the result of this.

There is no doubt that many of our attempts to grasp things by means of thinking, fail; this is apparent not only in the history of science, but also in ordinary life; it is just that in the simple cases we usually encounter, the right concept replaces the wrong one so quickly that we seldom or never become aware of the latter.

When Kant speaks of "the synthetic unity of apperception" it is evident that he had some inkling of what we have shown here to be an activity of thinking, the purpose of which is to organize the world-content systematically. But the fact that he believed that the a priori laws of pure science could be derived from the rules according to which this synthesis takes place, shows how little this inkling brought to his consciousness the essential task of thinking. He did not realize that this synthetic activity of thinking is only a *preparation* for discovering natural laws as such. Suppose, for example, that we detach one content, a, from the world-picture, and likewise another, b. If we are to gain knowledge of the law connecting a and b, then thinking must first relate a to b so that through this relationship the connection between them presents itself as given. Therefore, the actual content of a law of nature is derived from the given, and the task of thinking is merely to provide the opportunity for relating the elements of the world-picture so that the laws connecting them come to light. Thus there is no question of objective laws resulting from the synthetic activity of thinking alone.

We must now ask what part thinking plays in building up our scientific world-picture, in contrast to the merely given world-picture. Our discussion shows that thinking provides the thought-forms to which the laws that govern the world correspond. In the example given above, let us assume a to be the cause and b the effect. The fact that a and b are causally connected could never become knowledge if thinking were not able to form the concept of causality. Yet in order to recognize, in a given case, that *a* is the cause and *b* the effect, it is necessary for *a* and *b* to correspond to what we understand by cause and effect. And this is true of all other categories of thinking as well.

At this point it will be useful to refer briefly to Hume's description of the concept of causality. Hume said that our concepts of cause and effect are due solely to *habit*. We so often notice that a particular event is followed by another that accordingly we form the habit of thinking of them as causally connected, i.e. we expect the second event to occur whenever we observe the first. But this viewpoint stems from a mistaken representation of the relationship concerned in causality. Suppose that I always meet the same people every day for a number of days when I leave my house; it is true that I shall then gradually come to expect the two events to follow one another, but in this case it would never occur to me to look for a causal connection between the other persons and my own appearance at the same spot. I would look to quite different elements of the world-content in order to explain the facts involved. In fact, we never do determine a causal connection to be such from its sequence in time, but from its own content as part of the world-content which is that of cause and effect.

The activity of thinking is only a formal one in the up-building of our scientific world-picture, and from this it follows that no cognition can have a content which is a priori, in that it is established prior to observation (thinking divorced from the given); rather must the content be acquired wholly through observation. In this sense all our knowledge is empirical. Nor is it possible to see how this could be otherwise. Kant's judgments a priori fundamentally are not cognition, but are only postulates. In the Kantian sense, one can always only say: If a thing is to be the object of any kind of experience, then it must conform to certain laws. Laws in this sense are regulations which the subject prescribes for the objects. Yet one would expect that if we are to attain knowledge of the given then it must be derived, not from the subject, but from the object.

Thinking says nothing a priori about the given; it produces a posteriori, i.e. the thought-form, on the basis of which the conformity to law of the phenomena becomes apparent.

Seen in this light, it is obvious that one can say nothing a priori about the degree of certainty of a judgment attained through cognition. For certainty, too, can be derived only from the given. To this it could be objected that observation only shows that some connection between phenomena once occurred, but *not* that such a connection *must* occur, and in similar cases always *will* occur. This assumption is also wrong. When I recognize some particular connection between elements of the world-picture, this connection is provided by these elements themselves; it is not something I think into them, but is an essential part of them, and must necessarily be present whenever the elements themselves are present.

Only if it is considered that scientific effort is merely a matter of combining facts of experience according to subjective principles which are quite external to the facts themselves,—only such an outlook could believe that *a* and *b* may be connected by one law to-day and by another to-morrow (John Stuart Mill).[109] Someone who recognizes that the laws of nature originate in the given and therefore themselves constitute the connection between the phenomena and determine them, will not describe laws discovered by observation as merely of comparative universality. This is not to assert that a natural law which at one stage we assume to be correct must therefore be universally valid as well. When a later event disproves a law, this does not imply that the law had only a limited validity when first discovered, but rather that we failed to ascertain it with complete accuracy. A true law of nature is simply the expression of a connection within the given world-picture, and it exists as little without the facts it governs as the facts exist without the law.

We have established that the nature of the activity of cognition is to permeate the given world-picture with concepts and ideas by means of thinking. What follows from this fact? If the directly-given were a totality, complete in itself, then such an elaboration of it by means of cognition would be both impossible and unnecessary. We should then simply accept the given as it is, and would be satisfied with it in that form. The act of cognition is possible only because the given contains something hidden; this hidden does *not* appear as long as we consider only its immediate aspect; the hidden aspect only reveals itself through the order that thinking brings into the given. In other words, what the given appears to be *before* it has been elaborated by thinking, is not its full totality.

This becomes clearer when we consider more closely the factors concerned in the act of cognition. The first of these is the given. That it is *given* is not a feature of the given, but is only an expression for its relation to the second factor in the act of cognition. Thus what the given is as such remains quite undecided by this definition. The second factor is the conceptual content of the given; it is found by thinking, in the act of cognition, to be necessarily connected with the given. Let us now ask: 1) Where is the division between given and concept? 2) And where are they united? The answers to both of these questions are undoubtedly to be found in the preceding discussion. The division occurs solely in the act of cognition. In the given they are united. This shows that the conceptual content must necessarily be a part of the given, and also that the act of cognition consists in re-uniting the two parts of the world-picture, which to begin with are given to cognition separated from each other. Therefore, the given world-picture becomes complete only through that other, indirect kind of given which is brought to it by thinking. The immediate aspect of the world-picture reveals itself as quite incomplete to begin with.

If, in the world-content, the thought-content were united with the given from the first, no knowledge would exist, and the need to go beyond the given would never arise. If, on the other hand, we were to produce the whole content of the world in and by means of thinking alone, no knowledge would exist either. What we ourselves pro-

duce we have no need to know. Knowledge therefore rests
upon the fact that the world-content is originally given
to us in incomplete form; it possesses another essential aspect, apart from what is directly present. This second
aspect of the world-content, which is not originally given,
is revealed through thinking. Therefore the content of
thinking, which appears to us to be something separate,
is not a sum of *empty* thought-forms, but comprises determinations (categories); however, in relation to the rest
of the world-content, these determinations represent the
organizing principle. *The world-content can be called
reality only in the form it attains when the two aspects of
it described above have been united through knowledge.*

vi

THEORY OF KNOWLEDGE FREE
OF ASSUMPTIONS AND
FICHTE'S SCIENCE OF KNOWLEDGE

W E HAVE NOW defined the idea of knowledge. In the act
of cognition this idea is directly given in human consciousness. Both outer and inner perceptions, as well as
its own presence are given directly to the "I," which is
the center of consciousness. (It is hardly necessary to say
that here "center" is not meant to denote a particular
theory of consciousness, but is used merely for the sake of
brevity in order to designate consciousness as a whole.)
The I feels a need to discover more in the given than is
directly contained in it. In contrast to the given world, a
second world—the world of thinking—rises up to meet
the I and the I unites the two through its own free decision,
producing what we have defined as the idea of knowledge.
Here we see the fundamental difference between the way
the concept and the directly given are united within human consciousness to form full reality, and the way they
are found united in the remainder of the world-content.
In the entire remainder of the world-picture we must

conceive an original union which is an inherent necessity; an artificial separation occurs only in relation to *knowledge* at the point where cognition begins; cognition then cancels out this separation once more, in accordance with the original nature of the objective world. But in human consciousness the situation is different. Here the union of the two factors of reality depends upon the activity of consciousness. In all other objects, the separation has no significance for the objects themselves, but only for knowledge. Their union is original and their separation is derived from the union. Cognition separates them only because its nature is such that it cannot grasp their union without having first separated them. But the concept and the given reality of consciousness are originally separated, and their union is derived from their original separation; this is why cognition has the character described here. Just because, in consciousness, idea and given are necessarily separated, for consciousness the whole of reality divides into these two factors; and again, just because consciousness can unite them only by its own activity, it can arrive at full *reality* only by performing the act of cognition. All other categories (ideas), whether or not they are grasped in cognition, are necessarily united with their corresponding forms of the given. But the idea of knowledge can be united with its corresponding given only by the activity of consciousness. Consciousness as *a reality* exists only if it produces itself. I believe that I have now cleared the ground sufficiently to enable us to understand Fichte's *Science of Knowledge* through recognition of the fundamental mistake contained in it. Of all Kant's successors, Fichte is the one who felt most keenly that only a theory of consciousness could provide the foundation for knowledge in any form, yet he never came to recognize why this is so. He felt that what I have called the second step in the theory of knowledge, and which I formulated as a postulate, must be actively performed by the I. This can be seen, for example, from these words:

"The science of knowledge, insofar as it is to be a systematic science, is built up in the same manner in which all possible sciences, insofar as they are systematic, are built up, that is, through a determination of freedom; which freedom, in the science of knowledge, is particularly determined: to become conscious of the general manner of acting of the intelligence. . . . By means of this free act, something which is in itself already form, namely, the necessary act of the intelligence, is taken up as content and put into a new form, that is, the form of knowledge or of consciousness. . . ."[110]

What does Fichte here mean by the "acting of intelligence" if we express in clear concepts what he dimly felt? Nothing other than the production of the idea of knowledge, taking place in consciousness. Had Fichte become clear about this, then he would have formulated the above principle as follows: A science of knowledge has the task of bringing to consciousness the act of cognition, insofar as it is still an unconscious activity of the I; it must show that to objectify the idea of knowledge is a necessary deed of the I.

In his attempt to define the activity of the I, Fichte comes to the conclusion: "The I as absolute subject is something, the being (essence) of which consists merely in postulating its own existence."[111] For Fichte, this postulation of the I is the primal unconditioned deed, "it is the basis of all consciousness."[112] Therefore, in Fichte's sense too, the I can begin to be active only through an absolute original decision. But for Fichte it is impossible to find the actual content for this original activity postulated by the I. He had nothing toward which this activity could be directed or by which it could be determined. The I is to do something, but *what* is it to do? Fichte did not formulate the concept of knowledge which the I must produce, and in consequence he strove in vain to define any further activity of the I beyond its original deed. In fact, he finally stated that to investigate any such further activity does not lie within the scope of theory. In his deduction of representation, he does not begin from any absolute activity of the I or of the not-I, but he starts from a state of determination which, at the same time, itself determines, because in his view nothing else is, or can be contained directly in consciousness. What in turn determines the state of determination is left completely undecided in his theory; and because of this uncertainty, one is forced beyond theory into practical application of the science of knowledge.[113] However, through this statement Fichte completely abolishes all cognition. For the practical activity of the I belongs to a different sphere altogether. The postulate which I put forward above can clearly be produced by the I only in an act which is free, which is not first determined; but when the I cognizes, the important point is that the decision to do so is directed toward producing the idea of cognition. No doubt the I can do much else through free decision. But if epistemology is to be the foundation of all knowledge, the decisive point is not to have a definition of an I that is *"free,"* but of an I that *"cognizes."* Fichte has allowed himself to be too much influenced by his subjective inclinations to present the freedom of the human personality in the clearest possible light. Harms, in his address, *On the Philosophy of Fichte,* (p. 15) rightly says: "His world-view is predominantly and exclusively ethical, and his theory of knowledge has no other feature." Cognition would have no task to fulfil whatever if all spheres of reality were given in their totality. But the I, so long as it has not been inserted by thinking into the systematic whole of the world-picture, also exists as something merely directly given, so that it does not suffice to point to its activity. Yet Fichte is of the opinion that where the I is concerned, all that is necessary is to *seek and find it.* "We have to *search for* the absolute, first, and unconditioned fundamental principle of human knowledge. It cannot be *proven* nor *determined* if it is to be absolute first principle."[114] We have seen that the only instance where proof and definitions are not required is in regard to the content of pure logic. The I, however, belongs to reality, where it is necessary to establish the presence of this or that category within the given. This Fichte does not do. And this is why he gave his science of knowledge a mistaken form. Zeller[115] remarks that the logical formulas by which Fichte attempts to arrive at the concept of the I only lightly hide his predetermined purpose to reach his goal at any cost, so that the I could become his starting point. These words refer to the first form in which Fichte presented his science of knowledge in 1794. When it is realized that, owing to the whole trend of his philosophy, Fichte could not be content with any starting point for knowledge other than an absolute decree, it becomes clear that he has only two possibilities for making this beginning appear intelligible. One possibility is to focus the attention on one or another of the empirical activities of consciousness, and then crystallize out the pure concept of the I by gradually stripping away everything that did not originally belong to consciousness. The other possibility is to start directly with the original activity of the I, and then to bring its nature to light through self-contemplation and self-observation. Fichte chose the first possibility at the beginning of his philosophical path, but gradually went over to the second.

On the basis of Kant's synthesis of "transcendental apperception"* Fichte came to the conclusion that the activity of the I consists entirely in combining the material of experience into the form of judgment. To judge means to combine predicate with subject. This is stated purely formally in the expression: $a = a$. This proposition could not be made if the unknown factor x which unites the two a's did not rest on an absolute ability of the I, to postulate. For the proposition does not mean a exists, but rather: if a exists, then so does a. In other words there is no question of postulating a absolutely. In order, therefore, to arrive at something which is valid in a quite straightforward way, the only possibility is to declare the

---

* The perception of an object involving the consciousness of the pure self as subject. (Translator)

act of postulating as such to be absolute. Therefore, while *a* is conditional *the postulation* of *a* is itself unconditional. This postulation, however, is a deed of the I. To the I is ascribed the absolute and unconditional ability to postulate. In the proposition $a = a$, one *a* is postulated only because the other *a* is already postulated, and indeed is postulated by the I. "If *a* is postulated in the I, then it is postulated, or then it is."[116] This connection is possible only on condition that there exists in the I something which is always constant, something that leads over from one *a* to the other. The above mentioned *x* is based on this constant element. The I which postulates the one *a* is the same as the I which postulates the other *a*. This means that $I = I$. This proposition expressed in the form of a judgment: If the I exists, then the I exists, is meaningless. The I is not postulated by presupposing another I; it presupposes itself. This means: the I simply is, absolutely and unconditionally. The hypothetical form of a judgment, which is the form of all judgments, when an absolute I is not presupposed, here is transformed into a principle of absolute existence: *I* simply *am*. Fichte also expresses this as follows: "The I originally and absolutely postulates its own being."[117] This whole deduction of Fichte's is clearly nothing but a kind of pedagogical discussion, the aim of which is to guide his reader to the point where knowledge of the unconditional activity of the I dawns in him. His aim is to bring the activity of the I emphatically home to the reader, for without this activity there is no I.

Let us now survey Fichte's line of thought once more. On closer inspection one sees that there is a break in its sequence; a break, indeed, of a kind that casts doubt upon the correctness of his view of the original deed of the I. What is essentially absolute when the I postulates? The judgment is made: If *a* exists, then so does *a*. The *a* is postulated by the I. There can, therefore, be no doubt about the postulation as such. But even if the I is unconditioned insofar as its own activity is concerned, nevertheless the I cannot but postulate *something*. It cannot postulate the "activity, as such, by itself," but only a definite activity. In short: the postulation must have a content. However, the I cannot derive this content from itself, for by itself it can do no more than eternally postulate its own postulation. Therefore there must be something which is produced by this postulation, by this absolute activity of the I. Unless the I sets to work on something given which it postulates, it can do *"nothing"* and hence *cannot* postulate either. Fichte's own principle actually shows this: The I postulates its existence. This existence is a category. This means we have arrived at our principle: The activity of the I is to postulate, as a free decision, the concepts and ideas of the given. Fichte arrives at his conclusion only because he unconsciously sets out to prove that the I "exists." Had he worked out the concept of cognition, he would then have arrived at the true starting point of a theory of knowledge, namely: *The I postulates cognition.* Because Fichte is not clear as to what it is that determines the activity of the I, he simply characterizes this activity as the postulation of being, of existence. In doing so, he also limits the absolute activity of the I. If the I is only unconditioned in its "postulation of existence," everything else the I does must be conditioned. But then, all possible ways to pass from what is unconditioned to the conditioned are blocked. If the I is unconditioned only in the one direction described, it immediately ceases to be possible for the I to postulate, through an absolute act, anything but its own being. This makes it necessary to indicate the basis on which all the other activities of the I depend. Fichte sought for this in vain, as we have already seen.

This is why he turned to the other of the two possibilities indicated for deducing the I. As early as 1797, in his *First Introduction to the Science of Knowledge,* he recommends self-observation as the right method for attaining knowledge of the essential being of the I:

"Be aware of yourself, withdraw your attention from all that surrounds you and turn it toward your inner being—this is the first demand that philosophy makes on the pupil. What is essential is not outside of you, but solely within yourself."[118]

To introduce the science of knowledge in this way is indeed a great advance on his earlier introduction. In self-observation, the activity of the I is actually seen, not one-sidedly turned in a particular direction, not as merely postulating existence, but revealing many aspects of itself as it strives to grasp the directly given world-content in thinking. Self-observation reveals the I engaged in the activity of building up the world-picture by combining the given with concepts. However, someone who has not elaborated the above considerations for himself—and who therefore does not know that the I only arrives at the full content of reality when it approaches the *given* with its thought-forms—for him, the process of knowledge appears to consist in spinning the world out of the I itself. This is why Fichte sees the world-picture more and more as a construction of the I. He emphasizes ever more strongly that for the science of knowledge it is essential to awaken the faculty for watching the I while it constructs the world. He who is able to do this appears to Fichte to be at a higher stage of knowledge than someone who is able to see only the construction, the finished product. He who considers only the world of objects does not recognize that they have first been created by the I. He who observes the I while it constructs, sees the *foundation* of the finished world-picture; he knows the means by which it has come into being, and it appears to him as the result of presuppositions which for him are given. Ordinary consciousness sees only what is postulated, what is in some way or other determined; it does not provide insight into the premises, into the reasons why something is postulated in just the way it is, and not otherwise. For Fichte it is the task of a completely new sense organ to mediate knowledge of these premises. This he expresses most clearly in his *Introductory Lecture to the Science of Knowledge,* delivered at Berlin University in the autumn of 1813:

"This science presupposes a completely new inner sense organ, through which a new world is revealed which does not exist for the ordinary man at all." "The world revealed by this new sense, and therefore also the sense itself, is so far clearly defined: it consists in seeing the premises on which is based the judgment that 'something *is*'; that is, seeing the *foundation* of existence which, just because it is the foundation, is in itself nothing else and cannot be defined."[119]

Here too, Fichte lacks clear insight into the content of the activity carried out by the I. And he never attained this insight. That is why his science of knowledge could never become what he intended it to be: a philosophical foundation for science in general in the form of a theory of knowledge. Had he once recognized that the activity of the I can only be *postulated* by the I itself, this insight would also have led him to see that the activity must likewise be determined by the I itself. This, however, can occur only by a content being given to the otherwise purely formal activity of the I. As this content must be introduced by the I itself into its otherwise quite undetermined activity, the activity as such must also be determined by the I itself in accordance with the I's own nature. Otherwise its activity could not be postulated by the I, but at most by a "thing-in-itself" within the I, whose instrument the I would be. Had Fichte attempted to discover how the I determines its own activity, he would have arrived at the concept of knowledge which is to be produced by the I. Fichte's science of knowledge proves that even the acutest thinker cannot successfully contribute to any field of knowledge if he is unable to come to the right thought-form (category, idea) which, when supplemented by the given, constitutes reality. Such a thinker is like a person to whom wonderful melodies are played, but he does not hear them because he lacks an ear for music. Consciousness, as given, can be described only by someone who knows how to take possession of the "idea of consciousness."

Fichte once came very near the truth. In his *Introduc-*

tion to the Science of Knowledge (1797), he says that there are two theoretical systems: dogmatism—in which the I is determined by the objects; and idealism—in which the objects are determined by the I. In his opinion both are possible world-views. Both are capable of being built up into a consistent system. But the adherents of dogmatism must renounce the independence of the I and make it dependent on the "thing-in-itself." For the adherents of idealism, the opposite is the case. Which of the two systems a philosopher is to choose, Fichte leaves completely to the preference of the individual. But if one wishes the I to retain its independence, then one will cease to believe in external things and devote oneself to *idealism*.

This line of thought fails to consider one thing, namely that the I cannot reach any choice or decision which has some real foundation if it does not presuppose something which enables it to do so. Everything determined by the I remains empty and without content if the I does not find something that is full of content and determined through and through, which then makes it possible for the I to determine the given and, in doing so, also enables it to choose between idealism and dogmatism. This something which is permeated with content through and through is, however, the world of thinking. And to determine the given by means of thinking is to *cognize*. No matter from what aspect Fichte is considered, we shall find that his line of thought gains power and life when we think of the activity of the I, which he presents as grey and empty of content, as filled and organized by what we have called the process of cognition.

The I is freely able to become active of itself, and therefore it can also produce the category of cognition through self-determination; in the rest of the world, by objective necessity the categories are connected with the given corresponding to them. It must be the task of ethics and metaphysics to investigate the nature of this free self-determination, on the basis of our theory of knowledge. These sciences will also have to discuss whether the I is able to objectify ideas other than those of cognition. The present discussion shows that the I is free when it cognizes, when it objectifies the ideas of cognition. For when the directly given and the thought-form belonging to it are united by the I in the process of cognition, then the union of these two elements of reality—which otherwise would forever remain separated in consciousness—can only take place through a free act.

Our discussion sheds a completely new light on critical idealism. Anyone who has acquainted himself intimately with Fichte's system will know that it was a point of vital importance for this philosopher to uphold the principle that nothing from the external world can enter the I, that nothing takes place in the I which is not originally postulated by the I itself. Yet it is beyond all doubt that no idealism can derive from the I that form of the world-content which is here described as the directly given. This form of the world-content can only be *given*; it can never be constructed out of thinking. One need only consider that if all the colors were given us with the exception of one single shade, even then we could not begin to provide that shade out of the I alone. We can form a picture of distant regions that we have never seen, provided we have once personally experienced, as given, the various elements needed to form the picture. Then, out of the single facts given us, we combine the picture according to given information. We should strive in vain to invent for ourselves even a single perceptual element that has never appeared within our sphere of the given. It is, however, one thing merely to be *aware* of the given world; it is quite another to recognize its essential nature. This latter, though intimately connected with the world-content, does not become clear to us unless we ourselves build up reality out of the given and the activity of thinking. The essential What of the given is postulated for the I only through the I itself. Yet the I would have no occasion to postulate within itself the nature of something given if it did not first find itself confronted by a completely undetermined given. Therefore, what is postulated by the I as the nature and being of the world is not postulated *without* the I, but *through* it.

The true shape is not the first in which reality comes before the I, but the shape the I gives it. That first shape, in fact, has no significance for the objective world; it is significant only as a basis for the process of cognition. Thus it is not *that* shape which the theory of knowledge gives to the world which is *subjective;* the subjective shape is that in which the I at first encounters it. If, like Volkelt and others, one wishes to call this given world "experience," then one will have to say: The world-picture which, owing to the constitution of our consciousness, appears to us in a subjective form as experience, is completed through knowledge to become what it really is.

Our theory of knowledge supplies the foundation for true idealism in the real sense of the word. It establishes the conviction that in thinking the essence of the world is mediated. Through thinking alone the relationship between the details of the world-content become manifest, be it the relation of the sun to the stone it warms, or the relation of the I to the external world. In thinking alone the element is given which determines all things in their relations to one another.

An objection which Kantianism could still bring forward would be that the definition of the given described above holds good in the end only *for the I*. To this I must reply that according to the view of the world outlined here, the division between I and external world, like all other divisions, is valid only within the given and from this it follows that the term "for the I" has no significance when things have been understood by thinking, because *thinking* unites all opposites. The I ceases to be seen as something separated from the external world when the world is permeated by thinking; it therefore no longer makes sense to speak of definitions as being valid *for the I only*.

vii

EPISTEMOLOGICAL CONCLUSION

WE HAVE ESTABLISHED that the theory of knowledge is a science of significance for all human knowledge. The theory of knowledge alone can explain to us the relationship which the contents of the various branches of knowledge have to the world. Combined with them it enables us to understand the world, to attain a world-view. We acquire positive insight through particular judgments; through the theory of knowledge we learn the value of this insight for reality. Because we have adhered strictly to this absolutely fundamental principle and have not evaluated any particular instances of knowledge in our discussion, we have transcended all onesided world-views. Onesidedness, as a rule, results from the fact that the enquiry, instead of first investigating the process of cognition itself, immediately approaches some object of this process. Our discussion has shown that in *dogmatism,* the "thing-in-itself" cannot be employed as its fundamental principle; similarly, in *subjective idealism,* the "I" cannot be fundamental, for the mutual relationship of these principles must first be defined by thinking. The "thing-in-

89

itself" and "I" cannot be defined by deriving one from the other; both must be defined by thinking in conformity with their character and relationship. The adherent of *scepticism* must cease to doubt the possibility of knowing the world, for there is no room for doubt in regard to the "given"—it is still untouched by all predicates later bestowed on it by means of cognition. Should the sceptic maintain that our *cognitive* thinking can never approach the world, he can only maintain this with the help of thinking, and in so doing refutes himself. Whoever attempts to establish doubt in thinking by means of thinking itself admits, by implication, that thinking contains a power strong enough to support a conviction. Lastly, our theory of knowledge transcends both onesided *empiricism* and onesided *rationalism* by uniting them at a *higher level*. In this way, justice is done to both. *Empiricism* is justified by showing that as far as *content* is concerned, all knowledge of the given is to be attained only through direct contact with the given. And it will be found that this view also does justice to *rationalism* in that thinking is declared to be both the *necessary* and the *only* mediator of knowledge.

The world-view which has the closest affinity to the one presented here, built up on epistemological foundations, is that of A. E. Biedermann.[120] But to establish his standpoint, Biedermann uses concepts which do not belong in a theory of knowledge at all. He works with concepts such as existence, substance, space, time, etc., without having first investigated the process of cognition alone. Instead of first establishing the fact that in the process of cognition, to begin with, two elements only are present—the given and thinking—he speaks of reality as *existing* in different forms. For example,[121] he says:

"Every content of consciousness contains two fundamental factors; *two kinds of existence* are given to us in it, and these opposites we designate as *physical* and *spiritual,* or as *bodily* and ideal." (¶15) "What exists in space and time is material, but the foundation of all processes of existence, the subject of life, this also exists, but as an ideal; it has ideal being." (¶19)

Such considerations do not belong in a theory of knowledge, but in metaphysics, which in turn can be established only by means of a theory of knowledge. Admittedly, much of what Biedermann maintains is very similar to what I maintain, but the *methods* used to arrive at this are utterly different. No reason to draw any direct comparison has thus arisen. Biedermann seeks to attain an epistemological standpoint by means of a few metaphysical axioms. The attempt here is to acquire insight into reality by observing the process of cognition.

And we believe that we have shown that all conflicts between world-views result from a tendency to attempt to attain knowledge of something objective (thing, I, consciousness, etc.) without having first gained a sufficiently exact knowledge of what alone can elucidate all knowledge: *the nature of knowledge itself.*

PRACTICAL CONCLUSION

THE AIM OF THE preceding discussion has been to throw light on the relationship between our cognizing personality and the objective world. What does the possession of knowledge and science mean for us? This was the question to which we sought the answer.

Our discussion has shown that the innermost core of the world comes to expression in our knowledge. The harmony of laws ruling throughout the universe shines forth in human cognition.

It is part of man's task to bring into the sphere of *apparent* reality the fundamental laws of the universe which, although they rule all existence, would never come to existence as such. The very nature of knowledge is that the world-foundation, which is not to be found as such in objective reality, is present in it. Our knowledge—pictorially expressed—is a gradual, living penetration into the world's foundation.

A conviction such as this must also necessarily throw light upon our comprehension of practical life.

Our *moral ideals* determine the whole character of our

conduct in life. Our moral ideals are ideas which we have of our task in life—in other words, the ideas we form of what we should bring about through our deeds.

Our action is part of the universal world-process. It is therefore also subject to the general laws of that world-process.

Whenever something takes place in the universe, two things must be distinguished: the *external* course the event follows in space and time, and the *inner* law ruling it.

To recognize this law in the sphere of human conduct is simply a special instance of cognition. This means that the insight we have gained concerning the nature of knowledge must be applicable here also. To know oneself to be at one with one's deeds means to possess, as knowledge, the moral concepts and ideals that correspond to the deeds. If we recognize these laws, then our deeds are also *our own* creations. In such instances the laws are not something given, that is, they are not outside the object in which the activity appears; they are the content of the object itself, engaged in living activity. The object in this case is our own I. If the I has really penetrated its deed with full insight, in conformity with its nature, then it also feels itself to be master. As long as this is not the case, the laws ruling the deed confront us as something foreign, *they* rule *us*; what we do is done under the compulsion they exert over us. If they are transformed from being a foreign entity into a deed completely originating within our own I, then the compulsion ceases. That which compelled us, has become our own being. The laws no longer rule *over* us; *in* us they rule over the deed issuing from our I. To carry out a deed under the influence of a law external to the person who brings the deed to realization, is a deed done in unfreedom. To carry out a deed ruled by a law that lies within the one who brings it about, is a deed done in freedom. *To recognize the laws of one's deeds, means to become conscious of one's own freedom.* Thus the process of knowledge is the process of development toward freedom.

Not all our deeds have this character. Often we do not possess knowledge of the laws governing our deeds. Such deeds form a part of our activity which is unfree. In contrast, there is that other part where we make ourselves completely at one with the laws. This is the *free* sphere. Only insofar as man is able to live in *this* sphere, can he be called *moral*. To transform the first sphere of our activity into one that has the character of the second is the task of every individual's development, as well as the task of mankind as a whole.

The most important problem of all human thinking is: *to understand man as a free personality, whose very foundation is himself.*

EDITORIAL AND REFERENCE NOTES

Compiled by
PAUL M. ALLEN

4. Eduard von Hartmann, *Phänomenologie des sittlichen Bewusstseins,* Phenomenology of Moral Consciousness, German ed. p. 451. Born 1842, von Hartmann was originally an officer in the Prussian army. Because of an illness, he retired from military service and took up an intensive study of philosophy. In 1869 his *Philosophie des Unbewussten* (Philosophy of the Unconscious) appeared, and made him famous almost overnight. Of the many other works he wrote, this book remained his most famous. Rudolf Steiner describes a personal impression of von Hartmann, whom he visited in Berlin in 1888 following a philosophical correspondence with him over some years. This account may be found in Chapter IX of Steiner's autobiography. Steiner's *Wahrheit und Wissenschaft* (Truth and Knowledge), published in this present volume, was dedicated to von Hartmann. The latter died in 1906.

5. In his *Atomistik des Willens,* Atomic Theory of Will, Ger. ed., Hamburg, 1891, 2 vols. p. 213. Robert Hamerling, the Austrian poet-philosopher was born March 24, 1830. He early showed ability in poetry, and although from poor parentage, the generosity of friends enabled him to attend the gymnasium in Vienna, and afterward the University there. In the revolutionary movements which swept Europe in 1848, Hamerling joined the student legion in the Vienna revolt. The collapse of the uprising in 1849 made it necessary for him to hide for a long time in order to escape arrest. Later he studied

natural science and philosophy. In 1855 he was appointed master at the gymnasium in Trieste. Many years of ill health caused him finally to retire on a government pension in 1866. In comparatively comfortable circumstances, Hamerling spent the remainder of his life in his home near Gratz, devoting himself to writing until his death on July 13, 1889. He is referred to as "one of the most remarkable poets of the Austrian school; his poems are full of life and color." His most popular work was *Ahasver in Rom,* Ahasver in Rome (1866), with Nero as principal character. *Der König von Sion,* The King of Zion, (1869) is generally considered to be his masterpiece. In 1888 his *Homunculus* appeared, and was reviewed with extensive comment by Rudolf Steiner. His *Amor und Psyche* was published in 1882; his novel *Aspasia* (1876), described Greek life in the age of Pericles. In 1870 his drama concerning the French Revolution, *Danton und Robespierre,* was published. Rudolf Steiner commented on this drama in his Speech and Drama Course given in 1924, and in fact, many references to Hamerling and his work appear in books and lectures by Rudolf Steiner, including the latter's autobiography.

7. Georg Wilhelm Friedrich Hegel (1770-1831). A voluminous literature on Hegel and Hegelian thought exists in English, including biographical studies, translations, and commentaries on his writings. Consult any standard encyclopedia for details.

13. Johann Gottlieb Fichte. Born in 1762, Fichte studied at Meissen, Pforta, Jena and Leipzig with the intention of becoming a clergyman. After a teaching position in Switzerland, and enroute to another in Poland, he met Kant, under whose influence he wrote his *Study for a Critique of All Revelation.* The printer neglected to place his name on the title-page, and people thought the work had been written by Kant. When the true identity of the author became known, Fichte was hailed as a philosopher of outstanding merit. He lectured at Jena, Berlin and Erlangen. In 1807 he was made Rector of the University of Berlin. His death in 1814 occurred when he was at the height of his fame. Rudolf Steiner made extensive reference to Fichte, basing his doctoral thesis (published in enlarged form in the present volume as *Truth and Knowledge*) on Fichte's scientific

teachings, but perhaps his most memorable study of Fichte's life and thought was contained in a public lecture given in Berlin on December 16, 1915: *The Spirit of Fichte Present in Our Midst.* See also note 77, below.

16. Johann Wolfgang von Goethe, born Frankfurt a.M., August 28, 1749. Poet, dramatist, scientist, traveler, state minister, etc., author of *Faust, Wilhelm Meister,* and many other works. Died in Weimar, March 22, 1832. In August 1781 the Grand Duchess Amalia of Saxe-Weimar founded the *Tiefurter Journal,* the Journal of Tiefurt, to which Goethe contributed at her invitation. When Rudolf Steiner was active as editor of the natural scientific writings of Goethe at the Goethe-Schiller Archives in Weimar, he published proof that the *Fragment über die Natur,* The Fragment concerning Nature, which had appeared in the Journal of Tiefurt was definitely to be attributed to Goethe (*Schriften der Goethe-Gesellschaft,* Publications of the Goethe Society, ed. by Bernhard Suphan, Weimar, Vol. VII, 1892, article by Rudolf Steiner). Thus, just 110 years after the Fragment had appeared, Rudolf Steiner showed its importance and its relationship to Goethe's work. In the edition of Goethe's works published by Prof. Joseph Kürschner (1853-1902) (the volumes of Goethe's natural scientific writings edited by Rudolf Steiner), the Fragment appears at the beginning of the essays "On Natural Science in General," Vol. XXXIV, p. 1. The Fragment appeared in an English translation with notes by George Adams under the title, *Nature—An Essay in Aphorisms,* Anthroposophical Quarterly, London, Vol. VII, No. 1, Easter, 1932, pp. 2-5. In his *Goethe's Conception of the World,* Rudolf Steiner describes this Fragment as "the essay in which the seeds of the later Goethean world-conception are already to be found. What is here expressed as dim feeling, later developed into clear, definite thought." In similar vein, George Witkowski in his well-known biography of Goethe (Leipzig, 1899) describes this Fragment as "the seed from which came all of Goethe's great thoughts about nature."

20. Friedrich Wilhelm Joseph von Schelling (1775-1854). Often referred to as the Proteus among philosophers, Schelling was noted for his ever-changing alertness and brightness of mind and expres-

sion. Goethe (see note 16, above) had a very high regard for him, and spoke of him as "the most congenial philosopher I know." Schelling had a profound influence among the thinkers of his time, including philosophers of France and England. His last years were dedicated to what he termed "positive philosophy," radically different from the philosophy of identity, the transcendental idealism, and the pantheistic tendencies of his earlier time. Rudolf Steiner made extensive reference to Schelling in his writings and lectures, on various occasions praising that philosopher's "important inspirations and suggestions for what must afterwards be said by Anthroposophy, directly out of spiritual vision, on many points of Christianity." Steiner further spoke of Schelling, "who really always made a significant impression whenever he appeared in public—the short, thick-set man, with the extremely impressive head, and eyes which even in extreme old age were sparkling with fire, for from his eyes there spoke the fire of Truth, the fire of Knowledge." (From a lecture given at Dornach, Switzerland, Sept. 16, 1924) Perhaps Steiner's greatest study of Schelling is to be found in his *Die Rätsel der Philosophie,* The Riddles of Philosophy, Vol. I, Ch. 7. For English translations of Schelling and further details on his life, see any standard encyclopedia.

27. Immanuel Kant, German philosopher, was born in Königsburg April 22, 1724. He entered the university there in 1740, enrolled for the study of mathematics and physics. His studies were interrupted by the death of his father, which left him in poverty. After he supported himself by tutoring for 9 years, the kindness of a friend enabled him to resume his studies, to graduate as a doctor and to qualify as a privatdocent. He occupied this position for 15 years. His lectures widened from physics to include much philosophy. Finally, after unsuccessful attempts, in 1770 he was given the chair of logic and metaphysics at Königsburg. In 1781 his *Kritik der reinen Vernunft,* Critique of Pure Reason appeared, and in 1783, his *Prolegomena.* After the appearance of the 2nd edition of the *Kritik* in 1787, Kant became famous everywhere in German intellectual circles, and his views were regarded as those of an oracle. From 1792-97 he was engaged in a struggle with the government concerning his religious views. In 1794 he withdrew from society, and

gave up all teaching except for one public lecture course on logic. In 1797 Kant terminated a teaching activity that had extended over 42 years. He died in Königsburg on February 12, 1804 near the end of his 80th year. Little more than five feet tall, deformed in his right shoulder, his chest almost concave, Kant had a weak constitution. He never married, and followed an unchanging program of activities from youth to old age. For example, he never failed to rise at 5 o'clock, studied for 2 hours, lectured for 2 more, and spent the rest of the morning at his desk. He dined at a restaurant and spent the afternoon in conversation with friends. He then walked for about an hour—a walk which for years followed exactly the same course— studied for 2 hours more, and retired between 9 and 10. He was a prolific reader, especially in history, science, travel, and philosophy. He knew English history and literature intimately, especially in the period of Queen Anne. He read little of Goethe or Schiller, but often re-read Voltaire and Rousseau. He had little interest in nature, and in 80 years never traveled more than 40 miles from his native Königsburg. For further biographical details, works and translations, consult any standard encyclopedia.

28. Otto Liebmann, *Zur Analysis der Wirklichkeit,* Contribution to the Analysis of Reality, Strassburg, 1880, p. 28. Otto Liebmann (1840-1912) was well known for his writings on Kant's philosophical world-view.

32. Johannes Peter Müller, German physiologist and comparative anatomist, born in Coblentz, July 14, 1801. He studied at the University of Bonn, and was appointed to a professorship in physiology there in 1826. In 1843 he accepted the call to the chair of anatomy and physiology at Berlin University, which position he held with great honor until his death, April 28, 1858. He did much research in physiology, particularly in relation to human speech and hearing. His great work was the *Handbuch der Physiologie des Menschen,* 1833-40. (The English translation was made by Dr. William Baly, publ. London 1842). This work opened a new period in the study of physiology, and Müller is considered the main figure in the developments in this field in the mid-19th century. In his *Handbuch* Müller developed an entirely new principle which he called "the

law of specific energy of sense substances." This he expressed as follows: "The kind of sensation following stimulation of a sensory nerve does not depend on the mode of stimulation, but upon the nature of the sense organ. Thus, light, pressure, or mechanical stimulation acting on the retina and optic nerve invariably produces luminous impressions." It is to this law that Steiner refers at this point.

34. Arthur Schopenhauer (1788-1860), *Die Welt als Wille und Vorstellung* The World as Will and Representation, Four Books, publ. 1819 by Brockhaus, Leipzig. (English translation by Haldane & Kemp, 1883) Ref. Book I, par. 1, Ger. ed. Biographical data and translations of Schopenhauer's works, as well as extensive commentaries on his ideas have been published in English translation. Consult any standard encyclopedia for details. Rudolf Steiner edited a collected edition of the writings of Schopenhauer, 12 vols. with introduction by Steiner, publ. 1894.

42. Emil DuBois-Reymond, German physiologist and educator. Born Berlin, November 7th, 1818, in 1836 he entered the University of Berlin, where his teacher was Johannes Müller (see note 32, above). In 1840 he became the latter's assistant in physiology. His great work was the study of animal electricity, and his famous book was *Researches on Animal Electricity*, 1848-84. For many years he exerted great influence as a teacher. In 1858, upon the death of Müller, he was appointed to the latter's chair in physiology. In 1851 he had been admitted to the Academy of Sciences in Berlin; in 1867 he became its permanent secretary. His closest friend after Müller's death was von Helmholtz, who also had been a student of Müller. DuBois-Reymond died in Berlin on November 26, 1896. Rudolf Steiner makes many references to his work in lectures and writings.

53. The Kant-Laplace primordial nebula. On Immanuel Kant, see note 27, above. Pierre Simon Marquis de Laplace (1749-1827), was a French mathematician and astronomer who, at the age of 24 was named "the Newton of France" for certain of his discoveries. In the years 1799-1825 his great work, the *Mécanique céleste,* which, as its author stated, "offers a complete solution of the great mechanical problem presented by the solar system," appeared in 5 volumes, pub-

lished in Paris. In his second great work, the *Exposition du système du monde*, Paris, 1796, appeared his statement of his famous "nebular hypothesis," the origins of which he seems to attribute to Buffon, apparently unaware that Immanuel Kant had at least partially anticipated him in his *Allgemeine Naturgeschichte*, General History of Nature, published in 1755. Rudolf Steiner's criticism of the Kant-Laplace theory of the primordial nebula may be found in various places in his lectures and writings.

54. Ernst Heinrich Haeckel (1834-1919), German biologist, originally a physician in Berlin, became *Privatdozent* at Jena, afterward extraordinary professor of comparative anatomy, later professor of zoology, a chair established for him at Jena. This position he occupied for 43 years with intervals for zoological travels to various parts of the world. When Darwin's *Origin of the Species* appeared in 1859, Haeckel was deeply influenced by it, so that he became "the apostle of Darwinish in Germany." Among Haeckel's famous books are his *General Morphology* (1866), *Natural History of Creation* (1867) and *Die Weltraetsel* (1899), English title, *The Riddle of the Universe*, publ. 1901. By his 60th birthday Haeckel had published 42 works of some 13,000 pages, plus many monographs. Rudolf Steiner knew Haeckel personally, and in his autobiography, Chapter 15, Steiner recorded a very interesting and perceptive impression of the great scientist. The "genealogical tree" of Haeckel to which Steiner refers is set forth in its original form in Haeckel's *General Morphology* and developed in his later writings.

65. David Hume (1711-1776), Scottish philosopher and historian. Albert Einstein wrote, "If one reads Hume's books, one is amazed that many sometimes highly esteemed philosophers after him have been able to write so much obscure stuff and even to find grateful readers for it. Hume has permanently influenced the development of the best philosophers who came after him." Among those influenced by Hume may be numbered Immanuel Kant, William James, George Santayana and Bertrand Russell. Hume's writings and biographical and critical works concerning him and his ideas can be located by consulting any standard encyclopedia.

68. Karl Julius Schröer was born in Pressburg in 1825. In 1867

he was made professor of Literature in the Technical College of Vienna. In addition to his lectures on the history of German poetry as such, he lectured on Goethe and Schiller, on Walther von der Vogelweide, on German Grammar and Speech, etc. Rudolf Steiner was a pupil of Schröer, and refers to him in detail in his autobiography and in lectures. It was Schröer who recommended Steiner to Prof. Kürschner for the position of editor of Goethe's natural scientific writings. (See note 16, above) Schröer died in Vienna in 1900, and Rudolf Steiner has left an unforgettable word portrait and estimate of him in his *Vom Menschenrätsel*, Riddles of Man, publ. Berlin, 1916.

69. From July 1884 to September 1890, Rudolf Steiner was active as tutor in the home of Ladislaus (1834-1905) and Pauline (1846-1916) Specht at Kolingasse 19, Vienna IX. He taught their four sons, Richard, Arthur, Otto and Ernst. Richard Specht (1870-1932) became a well-known author of many works including biographical studies of Gustav Mahler, Richard Strauss, Franz Werfel, Brahms and Beethoven. Steiner gives details of this pedagogical activity in his autobiography, Chapter VI.

70. Rosa Mayreder (1858-1938), Austrian writer, also known as a painter. Her entire life was passed in Vienna and surroundings. She was the author of a number of popular novels. In addition, she was active in the movement for woman suffrage in Austria, at one time sharing in the direction of the movement itself, and editing its periodical. She wrote the libretto for Hugo Wolf's only opera, *Der Corregidor* (1896). Rudolf Steiner refers to Rosa Mayreder in his autobiography, Chapter IX.

71. See Johannes Volkelt's *Erfahrung und Denken. Kritische Grundlegung der Erkenntnistheorie,* Experience and Thinking. Critical Foundation for a Theory of Cognition. Hamburg and Leipzig, 1886. (Johannes Volkelt 1848-1930, philosopher, professor at Leipzig.)

72. *Grundlinien einer Erkenntnistheorie der Goetheschen Weltanschauung, mit besonderer Rücksicht auf Schiller,* publ. in English translation by Olin D. Wannamaker, New York, 1950, under the title, "The Theory of Knowledge Implicit in Goethe's World-

Conception—Fundamental Outlines with Special Reference to Schiller." The first German edition published Berlin and Stuttgart, 1886, revised ed., Stuttgart, 1924, with new Foreword by the author. Other editions: Dornach, 1924; Dresden, 1936; Freiburg i. Br., 1949; Dornach, 1960.

73. Aristotle (384-322 B.C.): *Physica Auscultatio,* On Nature as Cause and Change, and the General Principles of Natural Science.

74. Raimon Lull (Raymond Lully), (c.1235-1315) Catalan author, mystic and missionary. Born Majorca. In 1266 a series of visions led to a marked change in his life and purpose. Spent 9 years studying Arabic in order to refute the heretical teachings current in his time. At Ronda he wrote his famous *Ars Major* and *Ars Generalis.* He made many journeys in France, Italy, North Africa in a burning crusade against the teachings of Mohammedanism. At Bougie, North Africa he was stoned outside the city walls and died on June 29, 1315.

75. biogenesis, the teaching that living organisms come from other living organisms, as opposed to abiogenesis. The author of the modern formulation of "the fundamental law of biogenesis" was Fritz Müller (1864). Haeckel (see note 54, above) called Müller's formulation "the biogenetic fundamental law," which can be stated briefly as the teaching that in its development from the egg to adult stage, the animal tends to pass through a series of stages which recapitulate the stages through which its ancestry passed in the development of the species from a primitive form. In other words, the development of the individual is a condensed expression of the development of the race.

76. The earliest statement of the law of mechanical theory of heat was formulated by the French physicist, Sadi Nicholas Lèonhard Carnot (1796-1832) in notes written about 1830, published by his brother in the latter's *Life of Sadi Carnot,* Paris, 1878. Further work in this direction was done by Ségun, Paris, 1839, by Julius Robert Mayer, c. 1842, and by J. P. Joule, who (1840-43) placed the mechanical theory of heat on a sound experimental basis.

Julius Robert Mayer (1814-1878), German physician and physicist, is the discoverer of the law of conservation of energy, which—

within limits of the data he obtained from experiments and reasoning—he applied "with great power and insight to the explanation of numerous physical phenomena."

77. On Fichte, see note 13, above. Rudolf Steiner's Inaugural Dissertation for his doctoral degree before the Faculty of Philosophy at the University of Rostock (Defense, beginning of May, 1891; Promotion, October 26, 1891) was titled *Die Grundfrage der Erkenntnistheorie mit besonderer Rücksicht auf Fichtes Wissenschaftslehre, usw,* The Fundamentals of a Theory of Cognition with Special Reference to Fichte's Scientific Teaching. When the thesis was published in book form, as it appears here in English translation, a Foreword and one chapter were added to the original by Rudolf Steiner. These latter are included in the present translation.

78. John Locke (1632-1704), English philosopher, scholar, chemist, student of meterology, practising physician, political advisor, traveler and author. For details on his life and thought, consult any standard encyclopedia.

79. see reference to Volkelt's book in note 71, above.

80. see note 27, on Kant, above.

81. p. 61 ff. of Kirchmann's German edition of Kant's *Kritik*. See Kant, *Critique of Pure Reason,* Introd. to 2nd edition, Sec. vi.

82. Kant, *Prolegomena,* Sec. v.

83. Kant, *Kritik,* p. 53 f. of the German ed. Introduction, Sec. iv.

84. Rehmke, Johannes: *Die Welt als Wahrnehmung und Begriff, usw.,* The World as Percept and Concept, etc., Berlin, 1880, p. 161 ff. of the German ed.

85. Refer to title given in note 28, above.

86. *Note by Rudolf Steiner:* This attempt, incidentally, is one which the objections of Robert Zimmermann (*Uber Kant's mathematisches Vorurteil und dessen Folgen,* On Kant's Mathematical Notions and their Results) show to be, if not altogether in error, at least highly questionable. (Robert Zimmermann, 1824-1898, was Pro-

fessor of Philosophy in the University of Vienna, 1861-95. His book on Aesthetics was published in 2 volumes, Vienna, 1870. Rudolf Steiner attended lectures by Zimmermann on fundamentals of ethics at the University of Vienna. Steiner's impressions of this great interpreter of Herbart's aesthetics are contained in the 3rd chapter of the former's autobiography.)

87. Kant, *Kritik,* Introduction to 2nd edition, Sec. ii.

88. See Kant's *Theorie der Erfahrung,* Theory of Experience, pp. 90, ff. of the German ed.

89. Kant, *Kritik,* p. 58, Sec. v.

90. Hermann Cohen (1842-1918), *Kants Theorie der Erfahrung,* Kant's Theory of Experience, Berlin, 1871, pp. 90 ff. of the German ed.

91. August Stadler (1850-1910), *Die Grundsätze der reinen Erkenntnistheorie in der Kantschen Philosophie,* The Principles of the Pure Theory of Cognition in the Philosophy of Kant, Leipzig, 1876, p. 76 f. of the German ed.

92. Volkelt, op. cit., p. 21, see note 71, above.

93. Otto Liebmann (1840-1912), *Analysis,* 1880, p. 211 ff. (see note 28, above); A. Holder, *Kantischen Erkenntnistheorie,* Kant's Theory of Cognition, Tübingen, 1874, p. 14 ff.; Wilhelm Windelband (1848-1915) *Phasen der Kantschen Lehre,* Phases of Kant's Theory, p. 239; F. Ueberweg, *System der Logik,* System of Logis, p. 380 f.; Eduard v. Hartmann (1842-1906), *Kritische Grundlegung,* Berlin, 1875, p. 142-172 of the 2nd German ed. (see note 4, above).

94. *Note by Rudolf Steiner: Geschichte der neueren Philosophie,* History of More Recent Philosophy, 1860, Vol. 5, p. 60. Volkelt is mistaken about Fischer when he says (*Kant's Erkenntnistheorie,* Kant's Theory of Cognition, p. 198 f.) that "it is not clear from the account by K. Fischer whether, in his opinion, Kant takes for granted only the psychological fact of the occurrence of universal and necessary judgments, but also their objective validity and truth." For, in the passage cited above, Fischer says that the main difficulty of the *Critique of Pure Reason* is to be found in the fact that "its basic

points rest on certain presuppositions," which "must be allowed if the remainder is to be valid." For Fischer, these presuppositions consist in that "first the fact of knowledge is affirmed," and then analysis reveals the cognitive faculties "by means of which the fact itself is explained."

95. Gottlob Ernst Schulze (1761-1833), *Aenesidemus*, Helmstädt, 1792.

96. On Schopenhauer, see note 34 above.

97. On von Hartmann, see note 4, above.

98. *Kritische Grundlegung*, by Hartmann, Berlin 1875, Foreword, p. 10 of the German ed.

99. Liebmann, *Zur Analysis*, p. 28 ff. of the German ed. See note 28, above.

100. Kant's *Erkenntnistheorie*, Theory of Knowledge, Sec. 1.

101. A. Dorner, *Das menschliche Erkennen, usw.*, Human Cognition, Berlin, 1887.

102. Julius Heinrich v. Kirchmann (1802-1884), *Die Lehre vom Wissen*, The Theory of Knowledge, Berlin, 1868.

103. E. L. Fischer, *Die Grundfragen der Erkenntnistheorie*, Basic Questions of the Theory of Cognition, Mainz 1887, p. 385.

104. C. Göring, *System der kritischen Philosophie*, System of Critical Philosophy, Leipzig, 1874, Part I, p. 257.

105. Johannes Müller (1801-1858), see note 32, above.

106. Hartmann's *Grundproblem*, p. 37 (see note 4, above).

107. A. Döring, article in *Philosophische Monatshefte*, Vol. XXVI, 1890, p. 390. publ. Heidelberg. Philosophical Monthly.

108. Hartmann, *Grundproblem*, p. 1. See note 4, above.

109. John Stewart Mill (1806-1873). A stern parent, James Mill taught his son Greek at the age of three, and at seven he studied Plato's dialogues. When he was eight he had to teach his sister Latin. His introduction to the utilitarian teachings of Bentham (the great-

est happiness to the greatest number) at the age of fifteen was decisive for his life. His great work, *System of Logic*, 1843, is the analysis of inductive proof. He was a great champion of human rights, and in the second half of the 19th century his influence throughout Europe was very great. Today it is recognized that—to use Mill's description of Bentham—"He was not a great philosopher but a great reformer in philosophy." For details on Mill's life and thought, consult any standard encyclopedia.

110. Fichte, *Sämtliche Werke,* Collected Works, Berlin, 1845, Vol. I, p. 71 f.

111. For fundamentals of the scientific teaching of Fichte, see his Collected Works, Berlin, 1845, Vol. I, p. 97.

112. *Ibid.* Vol. I, p. 91.

113. *Ibid.* Vol. I, p. 178.

114. *Ibid.* Vol. I, p. 91.

115. Eduard Zeller (1814-1908), *Geschichte der deutschen Philosophie seit Leibnitz,* History of German Philosophy Since Leibnitz, Munich, 1871-75, p. 605. Eduard Zeller studied and taught at Tübingen, later (1847) becoming professor of Theology at Bern, later (1849) professor of Theology, afterward of Philosophy at Marburg. In 1862 he was made professor of Philosophy at Heidelberg, afterward at Berlin to his retirement in 1895. His masterwork is the *Philosophie der Greichen,* Philosophy of the Greeks, 1844-52. He was recognized throughout the academic world for his learning and contributions to scholarship, and received many distinctions and honors. His *Philosophie der Greichen* has been transl. into English by S. F. Alleyne, 2 vols. 1881. In addition, an abridged version prepared by Zeller (1883) also appeared in English in 1896, as did a number of his other writings.

116. Fichte, *Sämtliche Werke,* Collected Works, Berlin, 1845, Vol. I, p. 94.

117. *Ibid.* Vol. I, p. 98.

118. *Ibid.* Vol. I, p. 422.

119. *J. G. Fichtes nachgelassene Werke,* J. G. Fichte's Posthumous Works, Edited by J. H. Fichte, Vol. I, Bonn, 1834, p. 4 and 16. *(Einleitungsvorlesungen in die Wissenschaftslehre,* Introductory Studies in the Scientific Teachings.)

120. *Note by Rudolf Steiner:* See his *Christliche Dogmatik,* Christian Dogmatics, 2nd edition, 1884-85, the epistemological arguments, Vol. 1. A complete discussion of his point of view has been provided by Eduard von Hartmann; see *Kritische Wanderungen durch die Philosophie der Gegenwart,* Critical Survey of Contemporary Philosophy, p. 200 ff.

121. opus cit., see note 120, above.

CPSIA information can be obtained at www.ICGtesting.com
233077LV00001B/57/A